"In the pursuit of preparing healthy foods, chefs Alfred and Patricia Salvador, award-winning culinary experts, and nutritionist Joannie Dobbs, Ph.D., have embarked on creating and publishing this cookbook of recipes which prove that low-fat cooking can be onolicious. It has been my pleasure and honor to know Alfred, Pat and Joannie through the Project Lean Hawai'i, Nutrition Interagency coalition activities. Chefs Alfred and Pat have enhanced several of Castle Medical Center's special events by providing their skills at demonstration cooking over the years. Their cookbook is an important step in providing the Pacific Rim with a healthier alternative. Congratulations and mahalo for sharing your culinary talents with us."

—Deanna Napualani Nakamura, R.D.
Hawai'i Dietetic Association President, 1995-97

"These days just about everyone knows about the dangers of our usual diet of high-fat and high-salt foods. Unfortunately, most people think the healthy alternatives are boring and flavorless. Not so. In their new cookbook, *Eating Well in Hawai'i*, Al and Patty Salvador have compiled a host of delicious, hearty, healthy recipes that are delectable and easy to prepare. Try it and see—you'll be delighted."

—Richard Chamberlain

Eating Well in Hawai'i
Fish & Poi Chefs' Low-Fat Recipes

Eating Well in Hawai'i
Fish & Poi Chefs' Low-Fat Recipes

by Executive Chefs Patricia Salvador, CCC, Alfred Salvador Jr.,
and Nutritionist Joannie Dobbs, Ph.D. C.N.S.

MUTUAL PUBLISHING

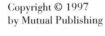

Library of Congress Catalog Card
Number: 97-73907

First Printing, October 1997
1 2 3 4 5 6 7 8 9

Casebound
ISBN 1-56647- 177-X

Cover Design by Jim Wageman/WIGWAG
Design by Mei Chi Chin

Mutual Publishing
1215 Center Street, Suite 210
Honolulu, Hawai'i 96816
Telephone (808) 732-1709
Fax (808) 734-4094
e-mail: mutual@lava.net

Printed in Taiwan

Dedication

We dedicate this book to our loving parents. Without their unconditional love, support and guidance, the co-authors could not be who they are and make this book possible. Our great aloha to our parents.

Raymond and Katherine Chu
Alfred, Sr. and Pacita Salvador
Peter and Helen Dobbs

Acknowledgements

A book is really the work of many people. The authors wish to express their gratitude for the assistance, information, support, cooperation, encouragement and friendship from the following individuals for their kokua in making this book possible.

We heartfully thank Lei Iwamura for typing, translation, and editorial assistance; Linda Davison for editorial corrections and suggestions; Suzi Pleyte and Claude Horan for many of the illustrations; Richard Viernes of Dole Ballroom for use of facilities, Gary Nelson of Orbit Sales for use of Steelite Dishes for Cover Photo; Ray Wong photographer and Vernon Lee assistant.

We would also like to thank Bennett Hymer, Jane Hopkins, Mei Chi Chin, and John Gibson of Mutual Publishing, for their support and expertise.

Very special friends: Richard Chamberlain, Jerry and Art Monnett, and Martin Rabbett.

Fish & Poi Chefs Members: with special thanks to Joe Kim, and John and Pat Tanaka.

Fish & Poi Chefs Assistants: Pat Nihi, Mat Silva, Julie Heatherly, Stacy Yamada, Rachael and Ruth Uu, Kea Nihi, Grace Kusuhara, Kenoalani Kamahele, Louie Dela Cruz, Ikaika Salvador, James Brian Salvador, and Kimo Chu.

Project LEAN Hawai'i, with the support of the Lyon Arboretum was instrumental in bringing chefs and nutritionists together for their Chef Showcase series demonstrating the preparation of low-fat cuisine. Some of the many individuals involved include: Ranjit Cooray of the Lyon Arboretum and his wife and Chef Kusuma Cooray, and nutritionists Alan Titchenal, Deanna Nakamura, Alice Toguchi-Matsuo, Alison Lum, Sharon Odum, Joda Derrickson, Trish Britten, Dian Dooley, Rosalind Philips, Serena Colah, and Robin Grondahl.

Culinary friends: Henry Vallejo, Vernon and Susan Wong, John Peru, Gordon Lum, William Trask, Rey Dasalla, Virgil Raquel, Jonathan Quiddaoen, Kris Vilassakdonand, Onjin Kim, Jim Davis, Mike Ellis, Ron Amasol, Derek Kajihiro, Alvin Beunafe, Menchie Eda, Amie Gordon, Gingerlee Pila, Gladys Sato, Chico Cera, Cory Iwanaka, Russell Hata, Grace Kusuhara, Thomas Mita, Wayne Matsumoto, James Nakata, Gale O'Malley, Bob Piccinino, Neil Aoki, Hans Weiler, Maurice Grasso, and Michael Ty.

Friends of the Media: Vinnie and Jessica Velapando - Filipino Beat; Diana Helfand The Heart-y Chef; HMSA Island Scene Magazine; Catherine Enomoto and Barbara Burke - Star Bulletin; Gary Nelson - Host Pacific Magazine; John Heckathorn - Honolulu Magazine; and Donna Shanefelter - Hawai'i Food Service News.

Health Organizations: HMSA Community Services; Don Weisman - American Heart Association; Vicki Suyat - formerly Hawai'i Diabetes Association; and Deanna Nakamura - Castle Medical Center.

Additional thanks go to Raymond and Katherine Chu; Shirley and Kiera Chu; Thomas Jr, Raylan, Thomas III, Mathew, Raymond, and Sherman Pung; Alan, Barbara and Robert Titchenal; and Dorothea and John Gaither.

Table of Contents

Recipe Table of Contents

* indicates the ingredient is in the glossary

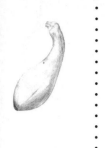

Pork, Veal, Beef ... 125

Vegetarian Dishes ... 143

Desserts 161

Foreword

Eating Well in Hawai'i—Fish & Poi Chefs' Low-fat Recipes promotes the idea that truly healthy eating must be pleasurable and this book demonstrates how you can make it that way. This book offers low-fat and healthy options to those of you who use and enjoy the wealth of knowledge and depth of experience hidden among its pages. Its depth may not be apparent to many who use it; this is what makes it a great work. It steers clear of the judgmental "good food/bad food" attitude and wisely incorporates the fact that nutrition is not a simplistic "black and white" science. Rather, it is a science of proportions and balance.

The formula for this book:
> Chefs + Nutritionist = Ultimate Flavor + Optimal Nutrition

Patricia and Alfred Salvador, Jr. are two chefs who happen to be married to each other. Born in Hawai'i and raised with its great depth and variety of multi-ethnic cuisine, they both have received too many awards in the culinary arts to count - local, national, and international.

Chefs Pat and Al have worked at all levels in their profession: as executive chefs, chef instructors, and personal chefs for international celebrities, to mention a few capacities. They frequently are seen volunteering their expertise for community fund-raising events, on TV promoting healthy cooking, and around the islands giving workshops on food, flavor, and feeling good.

Joannie Dobbs, Ph.D., C.N.S. is the nutritionist in the formula for this book. Her background is just as extensive. Joannie has worked as a student cook, hospital dietitian, and as a researcher conducting laboratory, wildlife, and human nutrition studies. She was one of the first nutritionists to work in computer programming for the nutrient analysis of diets and recipes.

Her knowledge of the nutrient composition of foods and the effects of food and nutrients on health is blended seamlessly with the culinary art of the chefs. Like the Salvadors, Joannie is actively involved in community service. She recently co-authored *Bone Appétit!, Calcium-rich Recipes for Healthy Bones* as a fund-raiser for the Hawai'i Osteoporosis Foundation.

As a sports nutritionist, I especially appreciate these recipes for their low-fat and frequently high carbohydrate content. This is the perfect support for an active lifestyle. Mix equal parts of physical activity (play) with a diet of these recipes and you get the balance that can promote optimal health.

Fortunately, you don't need to concern yourself with the many factors that came together to produce these recipes. You just need to enjoy them for their flavors and their benefits to your health.

These are not foods "to die for." These are truly foods "to live for!"

Alan Titchenal, Ph.D., C.N.S.
Sports Nutritionist
College of Tropical Agriculture and Human Resources
Department of Food Science & Human Nutrition
University of Hawai'i, Manoa

Also, Humble Husband of Dr. Dobbs

Authors' Preface

Our main goal is to have the general public understand that the quality of a person's health is determined by: Exercise, Frame of Mind, and a Proper Diet. With these recipes any individual can be on his/her way to eating and understanding what makes a healthy diet. This book is targeted towards teenagers, young singles, young married couples, "baby boomers", and retired people.

The recipes in this book are unique. All of the recipes meet the federal guidelines for low-fat and many meet the guidelines for Healthy as well. But don't let the low-fat stigma fool you into thinking that these are tasteless recipes. When fat was removed, other ingredients were added to insure a full flavor.

At first glance, some recipes may list more ingredients than you commonly use. When you review the list, you will notice that many of these are a teaspoon of this and a tablespoon of that. These extra ingredients are what puts the taste back into low-fat cooking.

The intention of this book was to create recipes for all ethnic groups. It is important for people to be familiar with the ingredients used. Ingredients unfamiliar to you may be fairly common in Hawai'i and in many cities throughout the continental United States. Most supermarkets have specialty food sections and most urban areas have gourmet food shops. Many kitchen supply stores also have different and unique foods for sale. In addition, there are growing numbers of mail-order gourmet food, spice, and beverage supply catalogs available.

The first step to a better quality of life is a more healthful diet, and the easiest way to take that first step is to enjoy the preparation and consumption of low-fat and healthy foods.

What is Fish & Poi Chefs?

Historically, the Hawaiian people were strong and physically fit. They ate fish from the ocean and poi from the land. Fish & Poi Chefs is a business owned and operated by two chefs, Patricia and Alfred Salvador, Jr. The name Fish & Poi Chefs relates to using all types of healthy food ingredients not just fish and poi.

In marriage, as well as in the culinary arts, Chef Pat and Chef Al realize the importance of harmony in relationships, in health, and in flavors. The philosophy of Fish & Poi Chefs includes the belief that food is more than just nourishment, but an important part of culture, tradition, and history.

Food can be our friend or our foe. Food can be an important partner in helping us to maintain good physical shape and to maintain a quality life as we grow older. Too much of the wrong types of foods can cause weight gain and influence our susceptibility to disease.

Research has shown a high correlation between good health and a low-fat diet. A crucial part of this relationship is eating a low-fat diet. This may sound a bit simplistic, however, over the past ten years there has been an overwhelming trend to producing low-fat foods that taste more like cardboard than food. The concept of "low-fat" meaning "tasteless" has been reinforced with every food we eat or recipe we make that doesn't meet our expectations.

Fish and Poi Chefs believes that an essential quality of any truly healthy food is for it to taste good. And if low-fat foods taste good, then including them in your diet becomes a pleasure rather than a penance. Chefs are trained in culinary techniques and the blending of flavors. Nutritionists, like Joannie Dobbs, are trained in food composition. The partnership between Fish and Poi Chefs and Joannie has focused on using the right combination of foods to produce low-fat foods with all the taste qualities of the higher-fat counterparts.

The recipes in this book were developed with six guidelines:
1. Good tasting food is essential.
2. All foods must meet the federal guidelines for low-fat.
3. Recipes must be easy to prepare.
4. Preparation time is realistic for most people.
5. Recipes must offer a variety of flavors and ethnic styles.
6. Ingredients must be available and affordable.

Diet-related disease can happen to anyone. Genetically, some people have a higher risk than others of heart disease, hypertension, cancer, and diabetes. Diet may not prevent these conditions, but it can delay them and in some cases reverse the symptoms.

The recipes in this book, like the people of Hawai'i, were influenced by cultures worldwide. Combining the best ingredients, flavors, and food styles often produce various ethnic foods with local flavors. And, whether you are a *kama'aina* (long time resident) or *malihini* (newcomer), young or old, you will find recipes to enjoy. These recipes were developed over two years and taste-tested by the public at hundreds of cooking demonstrations on O'ahu.

Although, the incentive for Fish & Poi Chefs began from a personal need to control blood cholesterol, the extension of their culinary skills to develop recipes and teach people how to prepare these foods has become a way of life. Fish & Poi Chefs want to be a part of the solution to diet-related illnesses by offering realistic and flavorful options.

This book is for you and the people you know. No one can predict the future or how long someone will live. However, with daily exercise, a good frame of mind, and a low-fat diet, most people will lower their risk of diet-related diseases and improve the quality of life as they get older. It is never too late or too early to start to take care of one's health.

Fish & Poi Chefs' motto is "Cooking with aloha for a healthier life." Now it is possible to have low-fat foods that add to the enjoyment of your life!

Ingredients Make the Taste

People eat out for many reasons: convenience, social aspects, no dishes to wash, atmosphere, and taste. And what makes restaurant foods taste so good? Ingredients and the way they are blended!

One of the key aspects of many restaurant ingredients is the freshness which then translates into fullness of flavor. Fresh fruits and vegetables have a number of qualities that make them special, such as crispness, natural sweetness, and eye appeal.

Fresh produce also boosts low-fat flavors without added sugar or salt. From the culinary standpoint, not having to consider differences in sweetness or saltiness of different food products allows more flexibility in combining them and makes it easier to create new flavors.

The recipes in this book were developed using fresh ingredients, unless otherwise stated. Frozen and canned ingredients can be substituted for fresh ones. However, taste may be altered and nutrient composition may be affected depending on the other ingredients added during processing. For example, fresh or frozen peas are naturally low in sodium, however, canned peas contain a significant amount of sodium.

For some, the convenience is as important as the flavor. If you have the time and the inclination to use fresh ingredients, we think the results are worth it. A word of caution, some people have said that fresh fruits and vegetables can become habit forming!

Why Nutrient Analysis?

Many of the links between diet and health have been known for some time. Thousands of studies have demonstrated the protective effects of lower fat diets. This, of course, is not news to those interested in this book.

There are now thousands of food products claiming to be low-fat or healthy. Many people have found choosing low-fat foods to be less than satisfying. This does not need to be the case.

The nutritional basis of the recipes in this book is not one of "good food/bad food." Good nutrition, including low-fat, is a matter of proportions and variety. It includes eating all types of foods in the right proportions. For example, whole eggs have been used in some recipes when the nutrient composition of the whole recipe still meets the definition for low-fat and has moderate or low levels of cholesterol.

"Low-fat" and "healthy" are not just buzz-words. All recipes in this book meet the Nutrition Labeling and Education Act (NLEA) guidelines for low-fat (3 grams of fat or less per serving for an individual food such as a soup, salad, or dessert). Main dishes or meals are allowed 3 grams of fat or less per 100 grams of food. In all cases, the saturated fat is limited.

Recipe titles marked with ❤ meet the NLEA definition for healthy, which includes restrictions for low-fat, saturated fat, cholesterol, sodium, percent of Calories from fat and saturated fat. The term "healthy" also requires that at least one "beneficial" nutrient (protein, fiber, calcium, iron, vitamin A or C) be included in specified amounts.

Nutrient analysis information is included for those who desire or require it to make food choices. The goal of including nutrient analysis information, along with diabetic exchange information, is to simplify food choices. Truly the focus should be on food rather than on nutrient numbers.

The Genesis R&D Nutrition Labeling and Formulation Software [ESHA Research, P.O. Box 13028, Salem OR 97309] was used to estimate the nutrient content of all recipes.

How to Use This Book

To assist you in the use of the cookbook and to insure that your recipes taste as good as the tested recipes in the cookbook, a number of conventions were followed.

1.   An asterisk (*) following a word indicates that the word is in the glossary.

2.   A ❤ following the recipe name indicates that the recipe also meets the strict definition for "healthy" as defined by the federal Nutrition Labeling and Education Act.

3.   Recipes consist of ingredients typically used in all types of cooking. Low-fat or nonfat items are used in recipes only when taste will not be compromised.

4.   Whenever possible, fresh ingredients are used in recipes, except when specified. Frozen ingredients can be substituted for fresh without altering nutritional composition greatly. If canned items are substituted for fresh, however, the sodium content in recipes will increase; sometimes significantly.

5.   Especially important to a full flavor are fresh herbs, fresh grated ginger, fresh citrus zest*, freshly milled/grated black pepper. When fresh herbs are not available, use the following conversions:

1 teaspoon fresh = 1/3 teaspoon dry = 1/10 teaspoon ground (dry)

6.   If the brand of a recipe ingredient is important to the taste, the preparation, or the level of nutritional composition, then the brand name or particular characteristics of the product will be discussed in the recipe. A brand name is not a promotion of the product but rather an indication that these products work in the recipe.

7.   Because fairly exact amounts of recipe ingredients are important to reproducing the right blend of flavors, most ingredients are expressed in measured amounts (ie. teaspoons, tablespoons, and cups) rather than in size amounts which may vary. For example: one person may think that a sliced medium-sized apple is equal to 1 cup, another person may think that it is equal to 1-1/2 cups, yet another may think it

is equal to 2 cups. Good measurements are also required to provide good approximations of nutrient content.

8.　Computer nutrient analysis is not an exact science but a good approximation tool for decision-making. Nutrient composition is slightly different for each food. It is also virtually impossible to measure every ingredient to an accuracy reported in many recipe books. Therefore, you will notice that nutrient values are rounded (550 mg sodium instead of 552 mg sodium). The rounding rules used were those recommended by the Nutrition Labeling and Education Act (NLEA).

9.　Vegetable oil sprays are used in a number of the recipes to limit the amount of fat in sautéing. We have listed the number of seconds of spray that will produce the nutrient analysis listed with each recipe. Generally 1 second of spray equals 1 gram of fat.

If you read the ingredient panel of non-stick sprays, you will notice that they are primarily oil. The nutrition fact labels indicate 0 grams of fat, but that is due to a quirk in the labeling act rather than the composition of the food. Dietary oils are fats.

10.　Because many people in America are concerned about their weight, the serving size for these recipes is based on reference amounts determined by the federal Nutrition Labeling and Education Act. In most cases, the serving number was based on the serving sizes which were customarily consumed during 1977-1978 and 1987-1988 nationwide Food Consumption Surveys conducted by the U.S. Department of Agriculture.

11.　Many people today like less salt in their food. Other people are on sodium-restricted diets. Because salt or soy sauce can be added easily to a recipe after completion, the recipes and analysis are based on less salt than you personally might prefer. Adding 1/4 teaspoon of salt adds approximately 500 mg sodium.

Soy sauce was used in many of the recipes both to enhance flavor and because it contains less sodium for taste than salt. If you would rather substitute salt for soy sauce or vice versa, you can adjust recipes using the following conversion information:

1/4 teaspoon Salt= 1-3/4 teaspoon Soy Sauce = 2-2/3 teaspoon "Lite" Soy Sauce

12.   Freshly ground black pepper or cracked black pepper add small explosions of flavor to food. Pre-ground black pepper, the pepper most of us have in our homes, gives a much different effect. To prevent confusion, the term milled black pepper refers to freshly ground or cracked black pepper.

13.   Tofu can be substituted for meat or poultry in many of the dishes. Keep in mind it will change the nutritional composition of the recipe. Because only lean meats have been used in these recipes, substituting regular or firm tofu will <u>increase</u> both the fat and Calorie content of the recipe.

14.   For those interested in knowing the percent Calories from fat, protein, or carbohydrate, these are listed on pages 211-221 along with the diabetic exchanges for each recipe.

15.   Diabetic Exchange Values
      Due to the use of many small amounts of various ingredients in recipes, diabetic exchange values in this book were frequently adjusted for nutrient content. When diabetic exchange values based on serving sizes did not accurately represent nutrient content, exchange numbers were adjusted to reflect actual nutrient content. For example, the highest priority was given to carbohydrate content so that exchange values closely match actual carbohydrate content of the recipe.

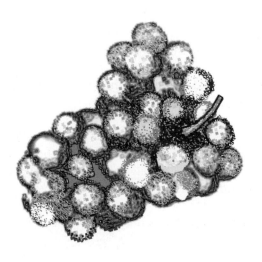

Low-Fat Cooking

It is very difficult to explain what makes great flavor in foods. But in our experience, food that is simply okay has either the wrong ingredient blend or has used the wrong cooking technique. We hope that reading through these pages and preparing these recipes will show you how simple low-fat cooking can be. You will understand the reasoning for using certain ingredients or removing other ingredients in preparing traditional types of recipes. We hope the few key factors in this chapter will give you confidence in "cooking like a pro." Eventually you will be converting your own family's favorite recipes and lowering the fat without sacrificing flavor.

Making Music

Cooking isn't really very complex. Actually it is very similar to the way a symphony makes great music: good instruments, good instructions, and a good conductor to coordinate the musicians. Just like a symphony, cooking involves precision, timing, and knowledge of how one ingredient will work in harmony with another. Keep in mind the volume or ratio of one ingredient to other ingredients changes the recipe, thus changing the flavor.

The instruments of a symphony are similar to ingredients used in cooking.
1) The soothing string section is the liquid ingredients (stocks, broths, wines, dairy, eggs, fats, and oils);
2) The dominant brass section is the aromatics and intense flavorings (herbs, garlic, peppers, spices, and sugars);
3) The mellowing sounds of the woodwinds and reed section are the fruits, vegetables, grains, pastas, and beans;
4) The bold and dainty percussion section is the meats, seafood, poultry and game.

The sheet music gives directions involving the melody and the tempo. The recipe gives directions involving cooking method, temperature, and length of cooking time. Of course the conductor and the cook make it all come together.

Now to play (cook) a melody (recipe)!

Let's start with a fast tempo (fire on high). Introduce the percussions (sear the beef), softly bring in the brass (adding garlic, herbs, seasoning). Now add just enough emphasis from woodwinds (adding onions, carrots and celery). Now soothing sounds of the string are heard (add your broth) and soon after the tempo slows (lower your heat to simmer). Right before the end you bring up the reeds and woodwinds (adding pearl barley). You might want to close with a little more of the brass section (adding a touch of seasoning). You just cooked beef barley soup.

Ingredients

Using the foods that we are used to is not only possible but we believe essential to successful low-fat cooking. New low-fat food items are introduced daily. Alone these foods may look and taste great, combined with other ingredients they may cause undesirable flavors to develop. In cooking, some nonfat items may not be good replacements for higher fat items.

Proportions

Proportions are as important as the ingredients themselves. One guideline is to use naturally low-fat ingredients (like fruits and vegetables) in abundance and high-fat ingredients (like butter, oils, cream, and meats) sparingly.

The first step to creating great tasting low-fat recipes is to start out with the right ingredients in the right proportions. Understanding the role these ingredients play in the flavor of that recipe will also help.

If the fat <u>does not</u> play a major role in the end flavor or is lost in the process of cooking, then most likely it could be decreased or eliminated. If the fat <u>does</u> play an important role in the recipe, then use it in moderation or use substitute ingredients. When the main flavor of a recipe is coming from strong spices, garlic, or wines, then you can accomplish the same flavor with evaporated skim milk and cornstarch as with heavy cream. Or if, a muffin recipe contains nuts, decrease the amount and sprinkle them on the top where they will be more easily tasted.

Vegetable Oil Sprays

A significant amount of dietary fat comes from cooking and salad oils (1 teaspoon equals about 5 grams of fat). Therefore, this book uses oils in the spray form to control the amount of fat in recipes. Nutrition fact panels indicate that vegetable oil sprays contain 0 grams of fat. This quirk of the labeling act is misleading and untrue, since these products are generally 100% fat. Although many vegetable oils are considered to be more healthful than animal fats, even vegetable oils, including those high in monounsaturated fatty acids, should be consumed in moderation. They are neither "bad" foods nor "health foods."

Substitutions

Understanding the role that each ingredient plays in a recipe makes it possible to substitute ingredients and still produce a low-fat recipe with lots of flavor. Heavy cream offers richness to sauces. This can often be replaced with evaporated skim milk and cornstarch and still maintain that quality of richness.

Sometimes removing one ingredient means replacing it with two. The fat in muffins plays two roles: 1) to maintain moistness and 2) to prevent sticking to the pan. Therefore to produce a low-fat muffin 1) use a pureed fruit like applesauce or prune paste for moistness and 2) use muffin paper or a vegetable oil spray to prevent sticking.

The most important rule for creating low-fat food substitutions is to make sure when you remove an ingredient that is essential for flavor, you add another ingredient with flavor back into the recipe. Without this, you will be assuring yourself of a taste failure.

Egg Substitutes

Not all egg substitutes or meat substitutes are created equal. Some egg substitutes remove the cholesterol but keep the fat, others remove both. It is not worth the expense to use the higher-fat substitute. This pertains to various meat substitutes (burgers and sausage links). Cholesterol-free does not necessarily imply low-fat.

Cooking Techniques and Equipment

There are many ways to cook the same food. For example, a fish could be sautéed, grilled, broiled, roasted, baked, smoked, pan-fried or deep-fried. The fish could also be steamed, stewed, poached, braised, microwaved, or stir-fried in a wok.

Most of these methods do not require the addition of fat. Only traditional pan- and deep-frying are not acceptable methods in low-fat cooking. However, with a few adjustments it is possible to cook foods that result in a fried flavor.

For example: french fries can be made by spraying dry french fry cut potatoes with canola oil and baking them on a sheet pan in an oven. It is important that the potatoes are dry to prevent steaming.

Sautéing is a hands-on quick way of cooking food. The food is turned rapidly to prevent sticking. The low-fat version is done easiest with a non-stick pan, however, a stainless steel, aluminum, or cast iron pan can be use if "seasoned" to prevent food from sticking.

To season a pan: with a paper towel, rub 1/4 cup of table salt into the interior of a clean pan. With a slight pressure, rub it evenly to produce a smooth surface; Lightly spray oil on the pan and rub it into the pores of the pan with a paper towel. Your pan is ready to sauté foods using little or no oil or butter. This low-fat style of cooking is called dry sauté.

Wok cooking, a common cooking method in Hawai'i, often adds a lot of oil to the cooking method. Adding small amounts of strong-flavored oils, like sesame or chili oil, is generally all that is necessary for a successful and flavorful food.

Food Safety

More than ever before, food safety needs to be stressed. Creating "low-fat" and "healthy" foods will do little good if certain rules of food safety are not followed. Here are a few common sense reminders for the three areas of food safety.

1) The Food
- Purchase the freshest food possible and never buy food which has an off-odor no matter how inexpensive it might be.
- Always wash produce to remove visible dirt, mud, bugs, and agricultural chemicals.
- If a can or bottle of food is bubbling or expanding, throw it away. Don't forget to make sure your pets can't get into it.

2) The Cook
- Wash your hands before handling food and throughout the food handling process.
- If you have a cut on your hand, use gloves.
- If a sick person in the family must cook, then make sure not to cough or sneeze over food. Wash hands often.
- If you touch your face or hair, wash your hands before touching the food again.
- Do not taste foods by dipping a finger into a sauce or re-using a spoon to taste food as ingredients are added.

3) The Kitchen
- Keep the kitchen clean.
- Keep refrigerator temperatures between 36 to 40 degrees F.
- Clean cutting boards thoroughly prior to cutting each new item.
- Keep all foods covered.

Drinks and Beverages

We begin this book with a 21 beverage salute to many great taste experiences and better health. Included are beverages for everyday and special occasions. In order to satisfy everyone's tastes, we've included a wide range of ingredients.

Today, the world's fruits and vegetables are available to us in many forms. We prefer fresh products because of the intensity of the flavors, but frozen and canned are also good options.

Often, a few subtle changes in diet can improve health as well as the overall feeling of well-being. We believe that the use of great tasting beverages, made from the "right" ingredients have a definite place in our lives. Some of these uses are:

- Quick and easy refreshment
- Simple low-Calorie refreshment and rehydration
- Full-flavored drinks replacing high-Calorie meals
- Increasing our intake of needed nutrients like antioxidants, vitamins, minerals, fiber, and electrolytes
- Expanding our taste sensations
- Celebrating a special occasion

Again we toast to better taste experiences and your better health.

Lemon-Lime Thirst-Quencher ♥

Makes 2 Servings

Hands On: 5 minutes

1 ½ cups chilled water

1 tablespoon fresh lemon juice

1 tablespoon fresh lime juice

2 lemon slices

2 lime slices

ice cubes

Combine chilled water, lemon juice, and lime juice in a quart pitcher.

Pour over ice in tall glasses.

Add lemon and lime slices to each glass and stir well.

Approximate Nutrient Content per Serving

Calories	10
Fat	0 g
Saturated Fat	0 g
Cholesterol	0 mg
Sodium	0 mg
Carbohydrate	3 g
Protein	0 g

Without added sugar, this thirst quencher is great after working in the yard or over a hot stove or anytime that you are really thirsty. Almost no calories - just refreshment.

Chef's Cocktail ❤

Hands On: 5 minutes

¹/₂ cup cranberry juice
¹/₂ cup club soda
1 lime wedge
crushed ice as needed

Mix cranberry juice and club soda in a tall glass.

Squeeze and drop lime wedge into juice.

Add crushed ice, stir and serve.

Approximate Nutrient Content per Serving

Calories	80
Fat	0 g
Saturated Fat	0 g
Cholesterol	0 mg
Sodium	30 mg
Carbohydrate	20 g
Protein	0 g

For a sweeter drink, use a lemon-lime soda in place of club soda or to keep Calories low, use a "diet" lemon-lime soda.

Maui Plantation Dazzle ❤

Hands On: 15 minutes
Unsupervised: 4 hours

2 cups water

¼ cup sugar

1 piece (1-inch) ginger*, bruised

2 tea bags

1 can (6-ounces) frozen pineapple* juice concentrate, thawed

¼ cup fresh lime juice

2 cups sparkling water

ice cubes

Combine water, sugar and ginger in saucepan. Bring to boil, reduce heat and simmer for 10 minutes.

Remove from heat, add tea bags and let stand for 10 minutes. Remove tea bags and ginger. Cool.

Pour into pitcher. Stir in pineapple concentrate and lime juice. Cover and chill for 4 hours.

Just before serving, stir in sparkling water and pour in tall glasses over ice.

Approximate Nutrient Content per Serving

Calories	150
Fat	0 g
Saturated Fat	0 g
Cholesterol	0 mg
Sodium	5 mg
Carbohydrate	38 g
Protein	1 g

The type of tea will influence the flavor of this drink. Try plain orange pekoe tea first, then experiment with other exotic flavors like hibiscus, pikake, or herbal.*

Kona-Sunset Frappé ♥

1 cup crushed ice

1 1/3 cup fresh orange juice

1/2 cup fresh lime juice

1 teaspoon maraschino cherry syrup

1 lime twist

Fill a cocktail shaker with ice. Add juices. Stir to chill.

Strain into a tall glass filled with ice.

Rub lime twist around rim of glass and drop twist on top of juice.

Drizzle cherry syrup on top and serve.

Approximate Nutrient Content per Serving

Calories	100
Fat	0 g
Saturated Fat	0 g
Cholesterol	0 mg
Sodium	0 mg
Carbohydrate	25 g
Protein	1 g

The name comes from the wonderful Kona orange, however, any full-flavored orange juice will work.

Physical Workout Spritz ❤

2 cups diced watermelon

1 cup diced Japanese pear*

1 kiwi*, peeled and quartered

8 medium strawberries, hulled, cut in half

2 cups chilled lime sparkling water

Combine watermelon, pear, kiwi, and strawberries in blender and puree until smooth.

Pour mixture into 4 tall glasses. Add 1/2 cup chilled sparkling water to each glass. Stir well and serve.

Approximate Nutrient Content per Serving

Calories	70
Fat	1 g
Saturated Fat	0 g
Cholesterol	0 mg
Sodium	0 mg
Carbohydrate	17 g
Protein	1 g

Choosing a sweet watermelon is not always easy. Thumping the melon only tells you if the melon is hollow or over-mature. The secret to choosing a sweet melon is an easy process. First, determine which end of the melon was attached to the vine and which was attached to the blossom. The smaller the indent on the blossom end, the sweeter the melon. The sweetest melons will have an indent as small as a pencil point.

Hawaiian-Honeymooners' Cocktail ♥

³/₄ cup passion fruit* juice, frozen in cubes

³/₄ cup pink lemonade, frozen in cubes

1 cup fresh orange juice

6 mint leaves

2 orange slices

2 maraschino cherries

Combine fruit juice cubes, orange juice, and mint in a blender. Puree until smooth and frothy.

Pour into a frosted stemmed tropical glass.

Garnish with orange slice and maraschino cherry and serve.

Approximate Nutrient Content per Serving

Calories	150
Fat	0 g
Saturated Fat	0 g
Cholesterol	0 mg
Sodium	10 mg
Carbohydrate	37 g
Protein	2 g

Placing the glass in the freezer for 20 minutes will frost it enough to add a wonderful sense of touch to this drink.

Mocha Nog ❤

$^1/_2$ cup prepared coffee, frozen in cubes

$^1/_3$ cup evaporated skim milk

I teaspoon sugar

2 teaspoons chocolate syrup*

I tablespoon wheat germ*

$^1/_8$ teaspoon fresh grated nutmeg

Combine coffee cubes, evaporated skim milk, sugar, chocolate syrup, and wheat germ in blender. Puree until smooth and frothy.

Pour into a tall glass. Top with nutmeg and serve.

Approximate Nutrient Content per Serving

Calories	140
Fat	I g
Saturated Fat	0 g
Cholesterol	5 mg
Sodium	110 mg
Carbohydrate	25 g
Protein	9 g

Freezing coffee is a great way to use your left-over coffee and give a great jump-start to a warm afternoon.

Christmas Cranberry Float ♥

Makes 6 Servings

Hands On: 5 minutes

1 can (12 ounces)
    cranraspberry juice
    frozen concentrate,
    thawed

4 cups lime sparkling water

3 cups crushed ice

2 cups lime sherbet

Combine cranraspberry concentrate and sparkling water in a 3-quart punch bowl.

Add crushed ice and sherbet.

Ladle mixture into tall chilled glasses. Serve immediately.

Approximate Nutrient Content per Serving

Calories	230
Fat	1.5 g
Saturated Fat	0.5 g
Cholesterol	5 mg
Sodium	35 mg
Carbohydrate	54 g
Protein	1 g

For a creamier drink, thaw sherbet in refrigerator for 15 to 20 minutes before combining with other ingredients.

Raspbango Tango ♥

2 cups diced mango*

1 cup apple juice

1 cup raspberry sorbet*

$^1/_2$ cup crushed ice

$^1/_2$ teaspoon milled black
   pepper*

Combine all ingredients into blender. Puree until smooth.

Pour into tall glasses and serve.

**Approximate Nutrient
Content per Serving**

Calories	240
Fat	0.5 g
Saturated Fat	0 g
Cholesterol	0 mg
Sodium	55 mg
Carbohydrate	60 g
Protein	2 g

The milled black pepper in this drink moves you to click you heels and do the tango.

Ikaika's Bionic Strawberry Defense ❤

Makes 2 Servings

Hands On: 10 minutes

1 cup sliced strawberries

$^1/_2$ cup peeled, sliced apples

$^1/_4$ cup peeled, sliced kiwi*

$^1/_3$ cup cubed mango*

$^1/_4$ cup strawberry low-fat yogurt

$^1/_2$ cup mango sorbet*

$^1/_2$ cup passion orange juice

1 $^1/_2$ cup crushed ice

Place all ingredients in blender and puree until smooth.

Pour into tall glasses and serve immediately.

Approximate Nutrient Content per Serving

Calories	180
Fat	1 g
Saturated Fat	0 g
Cholesterol	0 mg
Sodium	50 mg
Carbohydrate	43 g
Protein	3 g

This drink is the creation of Ikaika, the Salvador's 15-year old grandson. Ikaika loves strawberries and playing defense football.

James Brian's
Speckled Float ❤

$^1/_3$ cup sliced strawberries

$^1/_2$ cup sliced banana

1 cup root beer soda

$^1/_2$ cup crushed ice

1 tablespoon blueberry
low-fat yogurt

2 tablespoon Häagen
Dazs® "margarita
sorbet*

$^1/_2$ cup Post Fruity Pebbles®
Cereal

Place all ingredients, except cereal, in blender
and blend until smooth.

Add cereal to mixture in blender and blend
until specks of cereal are visible (about 2 minutes).

Pour into tall glasses and serve immediately.

**Approximate Nutrient
Content per Serving**

Calories	150
Fat	1 g
Saturated Fat	0 g
Cholesterol	0 mg
Sodium	70 mg
Carbohydrate	36 g
Protein	1 g

*Everything about this drink is fun, as might be
expected from the Salvador's 13-year old
grandson. The combination of ingredients show
great potential for creativity and dynamite
flavors.*

Matson Nectar ♥

Makes 2 Servings

Hands On: 15 minutes

1 cup fresh diced pineapple*

2 cups diced mango*

1 cup diced papaya*

³/₄ cup passion fruit* juice, frozen in cubes

4 mint leaves

Combine all ingredients into blender and puree until smooth.

Pour into tall glasses and serve.

Approximate Nutrient Content per Serving

Calories	220
Fat	1 g
Saturated Fat	0 g
Cholesterol	0 mg
Sodium	15 mg
Carbohydrate	57 g
Protein	2 g

For the ultimate flavor, use Hayden mangos. Haydens are in season in Hawai'i from May until August.

Puna Moon Eclipse ♥

1 cup pineapple* juice, frozen in cubes

8 hulled strawberries plus 2 for garnish

1 medium banana

²/₃ cup chilled skim milk

1 tablespoon coconut syrup*

2 tablespoons chocolate syrup*

Combine pineapple juice, 8 strawberries, banana, milk, and coconut syrup in a blender. Puree until smooth.

Pour one third of puree into 2 large stemmed cocktail glasses. Drizzle half of chocolate syrup over puree.

Finish drink by layering with puree, chocolate syrup, and remaining fruit puree.

Using a cocktail whisk or a pair of chopsticks, gently swirl mixture and chocolate. Garnish glass rim with a strawberry and serve.

Approximate Nutrient Content per Serving

Calories	260
Fat	2.5 g
Saturated Fat	1.5 g
Cholesterol	0 mg
Sodium	65 mg
Carbohydrate	60 g
Protein	5 g

This drink portrays the reddish tones that the moon over Puna and Kapoho takes on after fountains of lava erupt in the volcano area. The chocolate swirl represents the earth's shadow.

Old Homestead Mist ❤

2 medium star fruit*, diced

2 medium persimmons*, peeled and diced

1 cup passion orange juice, frozen in cubes

1 tablespoon crystallized ginger*

³/₄ cup vanilla low-fat yogurt

6 mint leaves

1 wet lemon peel*, julienne

4 slices of star fruit* for garnish

Combine diced star fruit, persimmons, fruit juice cubes, ginger, and low-fat yogurt. Puree until smooth.

Pour drink into stemmed glasses and top with lemon peel. Place sliced star fruit on glass rim as garnish and serve.

Approximate Nutrient Content per Serving

Calories	160
Fat	1 g
Saturated Fat	0 g
Cholesterol	0 mg
Sodium	40 mg
Carbohydrate	37 g
Protein	4 g

Crystallized ginger and wet lemon peel brings back memories of old homestead lifestyles. Fresh star fruit and persimmons are at peak season late fall to early winter.

Spark-of-Genius ♥

6 prickly pears*, peeled
    pressed through a sieve

12 seedless red grapes

3 kiwi*, peeled, quartered

$1/2$ cup guava* juice

$1/2$ cup pineapple* juice

$1 1/2$ cup crushed ice

Combine all ingredients in blender. Puree until ice is well blended.

Pour into tall glasses and serve.

Approximate Nutrient Content per Serving

Calories	150
Fat	1 g
Saturated Fat	0 g
Cholesterol	0 mg
Sodium	15 mg
Carbohydrate	36 g
Protein	2 g

Prickly pear is the fruit of the nopales cactus. This fruit is found abundantly in dry regions of the Big Island of Hawai'i in fall and winter.

Mango-Apricot Margarita

Makes 12 Servings

Hands On: 10 minutes
Unsupervised: 4 hours

3 cups diced mango*

6 cups apricot nectar

³/₄ cup frozen margarita
  concentrate mix,
  thawed

1 cup tequila

¹/₂ cup apricot brandy

4 cups crushed ice

lemon or lime slices

coarse salt, if desired

In a 4-quart non-metal container, combine mango, apricot nectar, margarita concentrate, tequila, brandy and ice.

Cover and freeze about 4 hours or until slush consistency, stirring occasionally.

At serving time, spoon only 3 cups of mixture into blender at a time and blend until desired consistency is reached.

To serve, rub rim of glass with lemon slices. Dip rim in coarse salt. Fill glasses.

**Approximate Nutrient
Content per Serving**

Calories	180
Fat	0 g
Saturated Fat	0 g
Cholesterol	0 mg
Sodium	5 mg without salt
Sodium	400 mg with salt
Carbohydrate	30 g
Protein	1 g

Do not let the fruity taste fool you. This drink has alcohol and it is potent.

White Lady Froth

Makes 2 Servings

Hands On: 10 minutes

1 cup diced pineapple*

2 cups peeled and seeded lychee*

2 tablespoons poha berry* preserve

1 cup vanilla low-fat frozen yogurt

1/4 cups gin

2 sprigs mint leaf

Combine all ingredients except mint sprigs in blender. Puree until smooth.

Pour into mai tai glasses and garnish with mint.

Approximate Nutrient Content per Serving

Calories	440
Fat	2.5 g
Saturated Fat	1 g
Cholesterol	5 mg
Sodium	70 mg
Carbohydrate	72 g
Protein	6 g

Fresh lychee and fresh pineapple are always better tasting. Madame Pele (also known as The White Lady) loves her gin, so this drink is definitely not for kids.

Sangria (Spanish Punch) ♥

¹/₂ cup lemon juice

¹/₂ cup orange juice

¹/₄ cup granulated sugar

3 cups non-alcoholic red wine

1 orange wedge

1 tablespoon granulated sugar

4 cups crushed ice

Mix lemon juice, orange juice, sugar, and non-alcoholic red wine.

Rub rim of 4 glasses with orange wedge. Place 1 tablespoon sugar into small dish. Dip the orange-rimmed glass in sugar.

Place crushed ice carefully into glass without disturbing sugared rim. Gently pour punch mixture into glasses ³/₄-inch from the top.

Serve immediately.

Approximate Nutrient Content per Serving

Calories	90
Fat	0 g
Saturated Fat	0 g
Cholesterol	0 mg
Sodium	15 mg
Carbohydrate	24 g
Protein	1 g

The zesty fresh flavor drink is perfect for a warm afternoon baby shower cocktail.

Kilauea Iki Blast ♥

1 lime, peeled

3 cups halved tomatoes

1 celery stalk, cut into
   1-inch pieces

$^1/_2$ cup green bell pepper,
   1-inch pieces

2 cloves garlic, peeled

1 teaspoon Tabasco

1 teaspoon Worcestershire

3 tablespoons plain low-fat
   yogurt

1 cup crushed ice

1 sprig parsley

Combine all ingredients into blender. Puree until smooth.

Pour into large fluted cocktail glasses and serve.

**Approximate Nutrient
Content per Serving**

Calories	100
Fat	1.5 g
Saturated Fat	0 g
Cholesterol	0 mg
Sodium	105 mg
Carbohydrate	22 g
Protein	4 g

This fiery drink is a wonderful way to "drink your vegetables".

Vegetable Perk-Me-Up ♥

Makes 2 Servings

Hands On: 10 minutes
Unsupervised: 2 hours

6 medium radishes

1 medium cucumber, peeled and seeded

3 cups peeled and seeded tomatoes

2 cloves garlic

1 medium beet, peeled and diced

1 cup shredded cabbage

1 teaspoon lemon juice

$1/_2$ teaspoon Tabasco

$1/_2$ teaspoon Worcestershire

Combine all ingredients in blender. Puree until smooth.

Pour into pitcher, chill for 2 hours. Stir before serving.

Approximate Nutrient Content per Serving

Calories	110
Fat	1.5 g
Saturated Fat	0 g
Cholesterol	0 mg
Sodium	90 mg
Carbohydrate	24 g
Protein	5 g

Beets naturally add the sweetness to this drink, therefore no sugar is needed.

Creamed Field of Greens

Makes 2 Servings

Hands On: 10 minutes

2 cups fresh spinach

$^1/_2$ cup chopped fresh basil

$^1/_2$ cup chopped celery

1 cup peeled and cucumber

$^1/_2$ cup green bell pepper slices

5 brussels sprouts

1 cup evaporated skim milk

$^1/_2$ teaspoon salt

$^1/_2$ teaspoon white pepper

1 tablespoon chopped toasted pumpkin seeds

Combine all ingredients, except pumpkin seeds, in blender. Puree until smooth.

Pour into 2 glasses and garnish top with pumpkin seeds.

Approximate Nutrient Content per Serving

Calories	160
Fat	1 g
Saturated Fat	0 g
Cholesterol	5 mg
Sodium	760 mg
Carbohydrate	27 g
Protein	14 g

Evaporated skim milk gives this drink a creamy texture without the fat.

Breads

The history of breads started before the recorded history of mankind. Breads have played an important role in civilizations from ancient times. Countries and cultures pride themselves on their unique breads, using ingredients indigenous to their region. Breads reflect cultural history, religion, superstition, climate and lifestyle.

Breads and bread products can be very quick to make or time consuming. They can contain only basic ingredients or be filled with delectable "goodies." Breads can be considered an appetizer, a main ingredient in a meal, a snack, or a dessert. In all cases, breads provide important nutrients.

Often flavor and moistness are incorporated into breads by adding butter or oils. To achieve the same results, we use a combination of other ingredients, like applesauce, prune paste, pureed baby food, fat-free egg substitute, and other low-fat items now available in supermarkets.

Substituting ingredients is generally not enough to make low-fat bread products taste good, so we've added the needed taste accent to "wake-up" your taste buds, for example jalapeño peppers in the corn muffins.

We feel that these bread recipes will add a positive aspect to the history of breads.

Cornmeal Muffins with Honey ❤

Makes 12 medium-size muffins

Hands On: 10 minutes
Unsupervised: 20 minutes

1 cup all purpose-flour

1 cup yellow cornmeal

1-1/2 tablespoons baking powder

1/2 teaspoon salt

1/2 cup fat-free egg substitute

1/3 cup 1% low-fat milk

2 tablespoons canola oil

1 cup canned creamed corn

1 tablespoon diced pimentos

1 tablespoon orange zest*

1 tablespoon grated low-fat Swiss cheese

1 jalapeño pepper, finely minced

2 tablespoons honey

Preheat oven to 400 degrees F.

Combine flour, cornmeal, baking powder, and salt. Set aside.

In another bowl, beat egg substitute, milk, and oil.

Add wet mixture to dry mixture and fold until smooth.

Add creamed corn, pimentos, orange zest, cheese, and jalapeño pepper. Fold until evenly mixed.

Line muffin tin with paper cups. Fill muffin cup 2/3 full with batter. Bake for 15 to 20 minutes.

Remove muffins from pan and drizzle honey on top of muffins while still hot. Serve warm.

Approximate Nutrient Content per Serving

Calories	140
Fat	3 g
Saturated Fat	0 g
Cholesterol	0 mg
Sodium	350 mg
Carbohydrate	24 g
Protein	4 g

Cornmeal muffins are usually very high in fat. The jalapeño pepper in this recipe gives this muffin lots of flavor while staying low in fat. This is a great muffin to accompany a lunch or dinner.

Orange-Cranberry Scones

Makes 12 Servings

Hands On: 10 minutes
Unsupervised: 15 minutes

2 cups all-purpose flour
plus 2 tablespoons for
work surface

$^1/_2$ teaspoon salt

$2^1/_2$ teaspoon baking
powder

$^1/_4$ cup sugar

$^1/_2$ cup dried cranberries

2 tablespoons orange zest*

$^1/_2$ cup applesauce

1 tablespoon butter

1 egg

1/4 cup skim milk

Preheat oven to 425 degrees F.

Combine flour, salt, baking powder, sugar, cranberries, and orange zest. Set aside.

In another bowl, whisk applesauce, butter, egg, and milk. Add wet mixture to dry ingredients, stirring gently with a fork.

Gather dough and place on lightly floured surface and gently knead 2 to 3 strokes. Roll dough out to $^1/_4$-inch thick. Cut with floured biscuit cutter. Place on baking sheet 1-inch apart. Bake for 12 to 15 minutes. Serve hot.

**Approximate Nutrient
Content per Serving**

Calories	140
Fat	2 g
Saturated Fat	1 g
Cholesterol	25 mg
Sodium	210 mg
Carbohydrate	27 g
Protein	3 g

Scones are similar to our American biscuits. Two things help achieve a light texture: 1. Do not over mix dough and 2. Use as little flour as possible on surface when kneading and rolling out the dough.

Lemon Tea Bread

Hands On: 15 minutes
Unsupervised: 70 minutes

2½ cups all-purpose flour

1 tablespoon baking powder

½ teaspoon salt

6 ounces light cream cheese, softened

⅔ cup applesauce

1 cup granulated sugar

2 egg whites

¾ cup skim milk

1½ tablespoons lemon zest* plus 1 teaspoon

¼ cup finely chopped toasted almonds

⅓ cup sifted powdered sugar

1 tablespoon fresh lemon juice

Preheat oven to 350 degrees F. Line two 8½ x 4½-inch loaf pans with parchment paper to cover bottom and sides.

Sift flour, baking powder, and salt. Set aside.

Beat cream cheese and applesauce until fluffy. Gradually add sugar and beat well. Add egg whites and beat well.

Alternate adding dry ingredients and milk to creamed mixture. Blend well. Fold in lemon zest and almonds.

Pour batter into pans. Bake for 45 to 50 minutes.

Combine powdered sugar, lemon juice and 1 teaspoon zest. Drizzle glaze over warm loaves. Let cool in pans for 15 minutes. Cool loaves completely on wire racks before cutting.

Approximate Nutrient Content per Serving

Calories	140
Fat	2.5 g
Saturated Fat	1 g
Cholesterol	5 mg
Sodium	180 mg
Carbohydrate	26 g
Protein	3 g

This quick bread recipe has a really nice, refreshing flavor. If fresh lemons are unavailable, use the juice and zest from an orange.

Mango-Banana Bread

Makes 22 Servings

Hands On: 15 minutes
Unsupervised: 1 hour

4 cups all-purpose flour

4 teaspoons baking soda

1 tablespoon salt

1 teaspoon cinnamon

1/4 teaspoon cloves

1/4 teaspoon nutmeg

1 1/2 cup sugar

5 large eggs

1 cup applesauce

2 teaspoons vanilla extract

1/4 cup chopped walnuts

2 cups mashed well-
ripened banana

2 cups diced mango*

Preheat oven to 350 degrees F. Line two 8 1/2 x 4 1/2-inch loaf pans with waxed paper to cover bottom and sides.

Combine in large bowl, flour, baking soda, salt, and spices.

In another bowl, combine sugar, eggs, applesauce, and vanilla. Mix well. Fold in walnuts, bananas, and mango.

Add wet ingredients to dry until blended well (3 to 5 minutes). Pour into lined loaf pans.

Bake for 1 hour. Remove from oven and cool on wire rack.

Approximate Nutrient Content per Serving

Calories	200
Fat	2.5 g
Saturated Fat	0.5 g
Cholesterol	50 mg
Sodium	540 mg
Carbohydrate	41 g
Protein	4 g

Twenty-four years ago, I made the original recipe with 1 cup of butter. Replacing the butter with applesauce, makes it just as moist and tasty, but with a lot less fat.

Pecan-Topped Pumpkin Bread ❤

Makes 20 Servings

Hands On: 15 minutes
Unsupervised: 1½ hours

3 cups sugar

½ cup applesauce

4 teaspoons canola oil

½ cup fat-free egg substitute

1 can (16-ounces) pumpkin

3 cups all-purpose flour plus 1 tablespoon for dusting

1 teaspoon cloves

1 teaspoon cinnamon

1 teaspoon nutmeg

1 teaspoon baking soda

½ teaspoon salt

½ teaspoon baking powder

⅓ cup chopped pecans

10 seconds vegetable oil spray

Preheat oven to 350 degrees F.

Beat sugar, applesauce, and oil in medium bowl. Add egg substitute and pumpkin. Mix well.

In separate bowl sift flour, cloves, cinnamon, nutmeg, baking soda, salt, and baking powder. Mix dry ingredients evenly. Make a well in flour mixture and pour pumpkin mixture into well folding with a wooden spatula. Mix evenly, but do not over mix.

Spray 8½ x 4½-inch loaf pans with vegetable oil spray and dust with flour. Pour batter into pans and sprinkle top of batter with pecans.

Bake for 1 hour and 10 minutes.

Remove from oven. Cool for 10 minutes, then remove from pans and cool completely on racks. Bread can then be wrapped air-tight and frozen.

Approximate Nutrient Content per Serving

Calories	240
Fat	3 g
Saturated Fat	0 g
Cholesterol	0 mg
Sodium	190 mg
Carbohydrate	52 g
Protein	3 g

The scent of cinnamon and cloves in the air makes this bread especially good during the holidays. Because it can be frozen, it can be readily available when unexpected guests arrive.

Apricot Bread ♥

Makes 20 Servings

Hands On: 15 minutes
Unsupervised: 1³/₄ hours

2 cups dried apricots
²/₃ cup golden raisins
4 cups all-purpose flour
4 teaspoons baking powder
1 teaspoon baking soda
1 teaspoon salt
1¹/₂ cups sugar
3 eggs
³/₄ cup applesauce
10 seconds vegetable oil spray

Soak apricots in hot water for 30 minutes. Drain and cut into strips. Soak raisins in hot water for 15 minutes and drain.

Preheat oven to 350 degrees F.

In large mixing bowl, combine flour, baking powder, baking soda, and salt.

In another bowl, cream sugar and eggs until pale yellow in color. Blend in applesauce, then apricots and raisins.

Pour wet mixture into dry ingredients and blend until smooth.

Spray two 8¹/₂ x 4¹/₂-inch loaf pans with vegetable oil spray. Pour batter into pans.

Bake for 1¹/₄ hour or until toothpick comes out clean.

Approximate Nutrient Content per Serving

Calories	220
Fat	1.5 g
Saturated Fat	0 g
Cholesterol	30 mg
Sodium	280 mg
Carbohydrate	48 g
Protein	4 g

This same batter can be spooned into muffin pans and baked at 350 degrees F for 25 minutes.

Boston Brown Bread

Hands On: 15 minutes
Unsupervised: 3 hours

½ cup whole wheat flour

¼ cup all-purpose flour

¼ cup yellow cornmeal

½ teaspoon baking powder

¼ teaspoon baking soda

¼ teaspoon salt

1 egg

¼ cup light molasses

3 tablespoons sugar

2 teaspoons canola oil

¾ cup buttermilk

¼ cup raisins

10 seconds vegetable oil
spray

Combine flours, cornmeal, baking powder, baking soda, and salt. Set aside.

In a large bowl, combine egg, molasses, sugar, and oil. Mix well.

Alternate adding dry ingredients and butter-milk to egg-molasses mixture. Mix in raisins.

Prepare two 16-ounces metal cans (about soup-can size) with vegetable oil spray and pour batter equally into cans. Cover cans with aluminum foil.

Put cans on a rack which is set in a covered roasting pan. Pour hot water into roasting pan to 1-inch of cans. Cover roasting pan and bring water to a boil on stove. Lower heat to simmer for 2½ to 3 hours. Add boiling water to roaster as water evaporates.

Remove cans from roaster. Let cool for 10 minutes. With can opener, cut bottom of can and remove bread. Serve warm.

**Approximate Nutrient
Content per Serving**

Calories	120
Fat	3 g
Saturated Fat	0 g
Cholesterol	20 mg
Sodium	1140 mg
Carbohydrate	23 g
Protein	3 g

This bread is a stove-top bread. It is very moist. For a darker bread, use dark molasses.

Bagels

Hands On: 35 minutes
Unsupervised: 40 minutes

4³/₄ cups all-purpose flour plus 1-2 tablespoons for work surface

2 packages active dry yeast (4 level teaspoons)

1¹/₂ cup lukewarm water

3 tablespoons sugar plus 1 tablespoon for boiling water

1 tablespoon salt

¹/₃ cup fat-free egg substitute

8 seconds vegetable oil spray

1 egg, beaten

In a large bowl, combine 1¹/₂ cups flour and yeast and make a well. In another mixing bowl, whisk together water, 3 tablespoons sugar, and salt. Pour wet into dry ingredients. Beat at low speed for a minute and then at high speed for 3 minutes. Stir in as much remaining flour as possible. When dough thickens, change to a dough hook or mix by hand with wooden spoon.

Turn dough on to lightly floured surface and knead until dough is stiff, smooth, and elastic. Cover with a clean close-woven cloth and rest dough for 10 minutes.

Divide dough into 12 portions, and shape each portion into a smooth ball. Make a hole (about 2-inches) in center of each ball and place on vegetable oil sprayed baking sheets, cover and let rise for 20 minutes.

Preheat oven to 375 degrees F. Bring 1 gallon water (plus 1 tablespoon sugar) to a boil; reduce heat to simmer. Boil 4 bagels at a time, turning once (total time about 7 minutes). Remove, drain, and brush top with egg. Place bagels on sprayed sheet pan. Bake for 25 to 30 minutes.

Approximate Nutrient Content per Serving

Calories	220
Fat	1.5 g
Saturated Fat	0 g
Cholesterol	20 mg
Sodium	550 mg
Carbohydrate	42 g
Protein	7 g

Sweet Potato Rolls ❤

Hands On: 20 minutes
Unsupervised: 90 minutes

3¹/₈ cups all-purpose flour

I cup whole wheat flour

2 packages active dry yeast
(about 4 level tea-
spoons)

4 tablespoons sugar

1¹/₄ teaspoon cinnamon

¹/₄ teaspoon cloves

¹/₄ teaspoon nutmeg

¹/₄ teaspoon salt

I cup skim milk

I cup canned unsweetened
sweet potato puree

2 tablespoons butter

¹/₄ cup applesauce

10 seconds vegetable oil
spray

2 eggs, beaten

Approximate Nutrient Content per Serving

Calories	140
Fat	2.5 g
Saturated Fat	1 g
Cholesterol	25 mg
Sodium	55 mg
Carbohydrate	25 g
Protein	4 g

Mix 1 cup all-purpose flour with whole wheat flour, yeast, 2 tablespoons sugar, 1 teaspoon cinnamon, cloves, nutmeg, and salt. Set aside.

In sauce pan combine milk, sweet potato, butter, and applesauce. When butter melts, beat sweet potato mixture into dry ingredients. Gradually add 2 cups of flour. Mix until a soft dough is formed.

Dust kneading surface with 1 tablespoon flour. Knead dough until smooth and elastic (about 10 minutes).

Lightly coat large bowl with vegetable oil spray. Place dough in bowl and cover with a clean close-woven cloth. Let dough rise about 1 hour or until it doubles in size.

Punch dough down and divide into 4 portions. Shape each portion into 5 balls. Coat a 13 x 9 x 2-inch baking pan with vegetable oil spray. Place 20 balls in pan, cover, let rise to double in size (30 minutes). Preheat oven at 350 degrees F.

Brush top of rolls with egg. Combine 2 tablespoons sugar and ¹/₄ teaspoon cinnamon and sprinkle over rolls. Bake for 20 minutes. Serve warm.

This roll is excellent for a late Sunday breakfast. By omitting the cinnamon and sugar topping, these rolls are also great with soups and stews.

Potato Bread ❤

Hands On: 20 minutes
Unsupervised: 2¹/₄ hours

1¹/₂ cups peeled and cubed
potato

1¹/₂ cups water

2 packages active dry yeast
(about 4 level tea-
spoons)

6¹/₂ cups all-purpose flour
plus 1-2 tablespoons for
work surface

3 tablespoons sugar

2 tablespoons vegetable
shortening

1 tablespoon salt

10 seconds vegetable oil
spray

1 tablespoon cornmeal

Simmer potato in water until cooked (about 12 minutes). Remove from heat. Allow potato to cool in water until potato is lukewarm. Set aside ¹/₂ cup of cooking liquid. Mash potato with enough remaining warm liquid to make 2 cups mashed potato mixture.

In a large mixing bowl, combine yeast and ¹/₂ cup potato water. Add mash potato mixture, 2 cups flour, sugar, shortening, and salt. Beat until well mixed.

Using a wooden spoon, gradually mix in flour until dough develops. Turn out onto floured surface and knead in remaining flour to make a stiff, smooth, and elastic dough. Shape into ball, place in lightly sprayed bowl, cover with a clean close-woven cloth. Let rise in warm, draft-free area until it doubles in size (about 1 hour).

Prepare two 8¹/₂ x 4¹/₂-inch loaf pans with spray. Punch dough down, turn out on floured surface. Divide dough in half and shape each into loaf. Cover, let rise until double (about 30 minutes). Preheat oven to 375 degrees F.

Brush top with water. Dust with cornmeal if desired. Bake for 40 to 45 minutes. Cover with foil the last 15 minutes of baking to prevent over-browning. Remove from pans and cool on racks.

**Approximate Nutrient
Content per Serving**

Calories	170
Fat	2 g
Saturated Fat	0 g
Cholesterol	0 mg
Sodium	290 mg
Carbohydrate	32 g
Protein	4 g

Kneading dough by hand allows you to feel when the dough reaches the perfect texture. Do not physically abuse your dough. Only light pressure from your palms is required to punch down and knead.

Russian Black Bread ❤

Hands On: 30 minutes
Unsupervised: 1³/₄ hours

4 cups all-purpose flour

4 cups dark rye flour

4 cups All Bran® cereal

2 packages active dry yeast

2 tablespoons caraway
seeds

1 tablespoon sugar

1 tablespoon fennel seeds,
crushed

1 tablespoon salt

3 cups water

¹/₃ cup molasses

1 ¹/₂ tablespoon butter

1 square (1-ounce)
unsweetened chocolate

2 tablespoons white
vinegar

1 tablespoon cornstarch

6 seconds vegetable oil
spray

Approximate Nutrient Content per Serving

Calories	230
Fat	3 g
Saturated Fat	1 g
Cholesterol	0 mg
Sodium	480 mg
Carbohydrate	50 g
Protein	8 g

In a large mixing bowl, combine 3 cups all-purpose flour, 1 cup rye flour, and add all remaining dry ingredients.

In a sauce pan, combine 2¹/₂ cups water, molasses, butter, chocolate, and vinegar. Heat until butter and chocolate are almost melted. Add liquid mixture to flour mixture. Beat well. Gradually add remaining rye flour and beat until well mixed.

Turn dough onto floured surface, knead in remaining all-purpose flour to form a stiff, smooth, elastic dough. Shape into ball, place in sprayed bowl (2 seconds), cover with a clean close-woven cloth and let rise until doubled in size (about 1 hour).

Punch down. Shape into 2 balls. Place onto sprayed baking sheets (2 seconds each). Flatten to a 6 to 7-inch diameter. Cover. Allow to rise until almost double in size (30 to 45 minutes). Preheat oven 375 degrees F.

Bake for 50 to 60 minutes. Remove from baking sheets and cool. Meanwhile, in a small sauce pan, heat remaining water and cornstarch until mixture becomes thick and clear. Brush over bread while still hot.

It is important to make sure that ingredients added to yeast mixture are not over 115 degrees F, otherwise yeast will die and bread will be flat and heavy.

Starters-Appetizers, Soups, and Salads

From the late 1930's until about the early 1980's, people who ate dinner out generally "dined." Dinner could last two to three hours, including an apéritif, appetizer, soup, salad, intermezzo, main course, dessert, coffees, liqueur chocolate cups, and sometimes even cigars. Often people ordered every course.

Today, our eating habits have changed. We seldom dine, but more often "catch something to eat" while racing from one place to another. Foods considered starters in the past are sometimes meals in themselves. And foods typically served as meals have become incorporated into appetizers, just served in smaller portions than the entrée.

A Starter course is intended to greet the diner and prepare him or her for a culinary experience. It should excite the senses, yet not take the spotlight away from the courses to follow. The volume served should be small. We hope that you enjoy these recipes and that they lead to great finales and curtain calls!

Marinated Green Mango Appetizer ♥

Makes 6 Servings

Hands On: 10 minutes
Unsupervised: 20 minutes

$^2/_3$ cup tomato juice

2 teaspoons minced garlic

$^1/_4$ cup chopped green bell
pepper

1 teaspoon lime juice

$^1/_2$ teaspoon hot chili paste*

1 tablespoon honey

1 teaspoon lime zest*

$^1/_4$ teaspoon milled black
pepper*

$2^1/_2$ cups thin strips of
green mango*

Garnish:

6 pieces of ti leaf* (4-inches
long)

18 whole fresh raspberries

6 slices of French bread
($^1/_4$-inch thick)

In a food processor or blender, puree tomato juice, garlic, bell pepper, lime juice, chili paste, and honey. Marinade should be smooth with bits of green pepper specks. Stir in lime zest and black pepper.

Place mango in shallow bowl. Pour marinade over mango and fold gently. Chill for at least 20 minutes.

For presentation, place ti leaf on a salad plate. Spoon $^1/_6$th of mango mixture over ti leaf.

Garnish with raspberries and serve with bread.

**Approximate Nutrient
Content per Serving**

Calories	150
Fat	1.5 g
Saturated Fat	0 g
Cholesterol	0 mg
Sodium	340 mg
Carbohydrate	32 g
Protein	4 g

If mangoes are taking too long to ripen, this is a great recipe for green or even half-ripe mangoes.

Cilantro Black Bean Dip with Pita Bread ❤

Makes 6 Servings

Hands On: 10 minutes
Unsupervised: 10 minutes

1 can (14 ounces) black beans, rinsed and drained

¹/₄ cup fat-free, reduced sodium chicken broth

1 tablespoon chopped cilantro*

2 teaspoons red wine vinegar

1 teaspoon lime juice

¹/₂ teaspoon Tabasco

¹/₂ cup diced red bell pepper

6 whole pita pockets

¹/₄ cup nonfat sour cream

1 teaspoon lime juice

sprig cilantro

Puree ³/₄ of beans, broth, cilantro, vinegar, lime juice, and Tabasco in a food processor. Scoop mixture into a mixing bowl. Fold in bell peppers and remaining black beans. Mix well. Spoon dip into serving bowl.

Cut each pita pocket into 8 wedges. Toast pita in oven for 5 to 10 minutes or until crisp.

In a second small bowl, combine sour cream and lime juice. Mix well. Spoon mixture in center of bean dip. Garnish with sprig of cilantro.

Place bowl with dip in center of large platter. Arrange pita wedges around the edge and serve.

Approximate Nutrient Content per Serving

Calories	220
Fat	1 g
Saturated Fat	0 g
Cholesterol	0 mg
Sodium	410 mg
Carbohydrate	42 g
Protein	10 g

Dips are quick and easy to make. Since appetizers are often very high in fat, this recipe is a good one. Whole wheat pita gives a heartier flavor.

Mushroom Quesadillas with Tomato-Pineapple Cilantro Salsa ❤

Makes 4 Servings

Hands On: 15 minutes
Unsupervised: 5 minutes

$3/_4$ cup Tomato-Pineapple Cilantro Salsa (next page)

4 seconds vegetable oil spray

5 ounces sliced mushrooms

2 cloves garlic, minced

2 fat-free wheat flour tortillas (8-inch diameter)

1 sliced round onion, separate rings

2 tablespoons chopped red onions

2 tablespoons chopped green onions

2 tablespoons chopped cilantro*

4 tablespoons shredded low-fat mozzarella cheese

Approximate Nutrient Content per Serving

Calories	110
Fat	3 g
Saturated Fat	0.5 g
Cholesterol	0 mg
Sodium	115 mg
Carbohydrate	17 g
Protein	4 g

Prepare Tomato-Pineapple Cilantro Salsa.

Lightly spray sauté pan with vegetable oil spray. Cook mushrooms and garlic on medium heat for 5 minutes. Remove from heat.

Preheat oven 350 degrees F.

Place 1 tortilla in an 8-inch ovenproof pan and heat to medium. Spread mushrooms evenly over tortilla. Sprinkle with all 3 onions, cilantro, and cheese. Cover with second tortilla. Turn quesadilla over to heat other side for 2 minutes.

Place quesadilla in oven for 5 minutes. Remove and cut into 8 wedges. Each hot wedge is served with a tablespoons of Tomato-Pineapple Cilantro salsa.

Regular parsley can be substituted for cilantro, if desired.

Tomato-Pineapple Cilantro Salsa ♥

Makes 1½ cups

Hands On: 10 minutes

1 cup diced, peeled and
    seeded tomato

⅓ cup finely diced pine-
    apple*

1 tablespoon chopped red
    onion

¼ cup finely diced yellow
    bell pepper

2 tablespoons white
    vinegar

1 teaspoon cumin

1 teaspoon minced garlic

2 teaspoons hot chili
    paste*

2 tablespoons chopped
    cilantro*

Combine all ingredients and refrigerate. Best if made one day ahead.

Approximate Nutrient Content per 2 tablespoons

Calories	10
Fat	0 g
Saturated Fat	0 g
Cholesterol	0 mg
Sodium	10 mg
Carbohydrate	2 g
Protein	0 g

Using fresh sugarloaf pineapple makes this a salsa to remember!

Crab Cakes with Pink Grapefruit Cream ♥

Makes 4 Servings

Hands On: 20 minutes

4 tablespoons Pink Grapefruit Cream (next page)

6 seconds vegetable oil spray

$1/_3$ cup minced onions

2 cloves garlic, minced

$1/_3$ cup minced celery

$1/_4$ cup minced red bell pepper

I cup corn kernels

I teaspoon lemon juice

I teaspoon Worcestershire

$1/_8$ teaspoon cayenne

$1/_2$ lb crab meat, chopped

$1/_4$ cup fat-free egg substitute

I tablespoon fat-free mayonnaise

I cup fresh bread crumbs

I tablespoon chopped parsley

4 butter lettuce leaves

4 lemon twists

2 teaspoons chopped parsley

Approximate Nutrient Content per Serving

Calories	170
Fat	3 g
Saturated Fat	0 g
Cholesterol	50 mg
Sodium	400 mg
Carbohydrate	19 g
Protein	16 g

Prepare Pink Grapefruit Cream.

Prepare sauté pan with vegetable oil spray. Sauté onions, garlic, celery, bell pepper, and corn until tender. Add lemon juice, Worcestershire, and cayenne; mix well. Transfer to a bowl, allow to cool slightly.

Add crab, egg substitute, and mayonnaise and fold together. Add crumbs and parsley, mix well. Shape into 4 patties.

Heat sauté pan and cook patties 3 to 4 minutes each side, turning over once. Patties should be evenly browned.

To serve, place warm crab cake on lettuce leaf. Drizzle 1 tablespoon Pink Grapefruit Creme around edge of patty. Garnish with lemon twist and parsley.

Day-old French bread is great to make the fine bread crumbs needed for this dish. Remove the crust and discard. Pulse bread in a food processor or chop fine with a knife.

Pink Grapefruit Creme

Makes 1³/₄ cups

Hands On: 10 minutes

1 cup fat-free mayonnaise

¹/₂ tablespoon pickled ginger*

1 teaspoon chopped cilantro*

¹/₂ cup pink grapefruit juice

¹/₄ cup peeled, seeded, and chopped tomato

¹/₂ tablespoon balsamic vinegar*

¹/₂ teaspoon chopped fresh basil

¹/₂ teaspoon chopped fresh dill

1 teaspoon capers*

¹/₂ teaspoon white pepper

In a food processor, combine mayonnaise, pickled ginger, cilantro, grapefruit juice, tomato, and vinegar. Blend until very smooth. Pour into a small bowl.

Add basil, dill, capers, and white pepper and mix well. Cover and chill until ready to serve.

Approximate Nutrient Content per 2 Tablespoons

Calories	15
Fat	0 g
Saturated Fat	0 g
Cholesterol	0 mg
Sodium	160 mg
Carbohydrate	3 g
Protein	0 g

This is a great replacement for tartar sauce. The recipe for pickled ginger, also known as Garni Shoga, is found in the Basic Recipe Section (page 195).

Spicy Chicken Soup with Lemon Grass ❤

2 cups fat-free, reduced sodium chicken broth

2¹⁄₂ cups water

1 stalk lemon grass*, sliced

¹⁄₂ cup straw mushrooms*, rinsed and drained

2 kaffir lime leaves*

1 cup thinly sliced carrot

1 tablespoon grated ginger*

¹⁄₂ pound skinless, boneless chicken breast, diced

¹⁄₄ cup fresh lime juice

2 Hawaiian chili peppers*, seeded and chopped

2 tablespoons chopped green onions

1 tablespoon chopped cilantro*

¹⁄₂ cup diced soft tofu*

1 tablespoon lime zest*

Cilantro sprigs

Approximate Nutrient Content per Serving

Calories	80
Fat	1.5 g
Saturated Fat	0 g
Cholesterol	20 mg
Sodium	310 mg
Carbohydrate	5 g
Protein	12 g

Bring broth and water to a boil. Add lemon grass, mushrooms, lime leaves, and carrot. Simmer 3 minutes and add ginger. Add chicken and simmer 4 minutes. Add lime juice, chili peppers, green onions, and cilantro.

Remove from heat. Garnish with tofu, lime zest and cilantro. Serve hot.

Lemon grass and kaffir lime leaves add the wonderful flavor to this soup. If you cannot find these ingredients in a supermarket or Asian store, look for them in nurseries as potted plants.

Kabocha Spinach Soup with Beef ♥

Makes 10 Servings

Hands On: 35 minutes
Unsupervised: 10 minutes

1 cup diced onion

4 cloves garlic, chopped

²/₃ cup diced celery

2 teaspoons canola oil

¹/₂ pound all-lean top round
beef, stew-cut

6 cups fat-free, reduced
sodium chicken broth

¹/₂ cup diced carrots

3 pounds kabocha squash*,
peeled and cubed

¹/₂ pound spinach, cut into
4-inch strips

¹/₂ teaspoon salt

¹/₄ teaspoon white pepper

Sauté onions, garlic, and celery in oil until vegetables begin to wilt. Add beef and brown evenly on all sides. Add broth and simmer for 15 minutes. Skim fat from surface.

Add carrots and simmer 5 minutes. Add squash and simmer 5 minutes; add spinach, salt, and pepper and simmer 5 more minutes.

Serve hot.

Approximate Nutrient Content per Serving

Calories	80
Fat	2 g
Saturated Fat	0 g
Cholesterol	15 mg
Sodium	480 mg
Carbohydrate	8 g
Protein	9 g

The safest way to cut and peel kabocha is over a cutting board. Cut down the center with a sharp knife. Remove seeds. Lay flat side of squash down on cutting board. With knife, slice outer skin down and away from you. Butternut squash is easier to peel and can be substituted for kabocha, although the color and flavor is not as good as kabocha.

Tortilla Soup

5 seconds vegetable oil spray

1 cup chopped onions

3 cloves garlic, diced

1 teaspoon taco seasoning

1 can (12 ounces) plum tomatoes

4 cups fat-free, reduced sodium chicken broth

3 corn tortillas (6-inch in diameter)

4 tablespoons low-fat sour cream

$1/_4$ cup diced green onions

2 teaspoons chopped cilantro*

6 lime wedges

Prepare bottom of stockpot with vegetable oil spray. Sauté onions and garlic until tender. Add taco seasoning and sauté for 3 more minutes.

Preheat oven to 350 degrees F.

Puree onion-garlic mixture with the tomatoes and broth. Return liquid to stockpot. Then simmer mixture for 20 minutes. Soup will reduce and thicken slightly.

Meanwhile, cut tortillas into 1 to 3-inch strips. Place strips on baking pan and lightly brown in oven (7 to 10 minutes).

To serve, ladle soup into 6 soup bowls, garnish with tortilla, sour cream, green onions, and cilantro. Serve lime wedges on the side.

Approximate Nutrient Content per Serving

Calories	100
Fat	2.5 g
Saturated Fat	1 g
Cholesterol	5 mg
Sodium	530 mg
Carbohydrate	15 g
Protein	4 g

Chayote and Watercress Soup

Makes 10 Servings

Hands On: 25 minutes
Unsupervised: 15 minutes

1 tablespoon butter

1 cup chopped onions

$1/2$ cup diced carrots

3 cloves garlic, chopped

2 stalks celery, chopped

8 cups fat-free, reduced sodium chicken broth

4 medium size chayote*, peeled and chopped

$1/2$ pound cleaned chopped watercress*

$1/2$ teaspoon salt

$1/2$ teaspoon white pepper

$1/4$ teaspoon nutmeg

$1/2$ cup thin strips of seeded tomato

watercress sprig to garnish

Heat butter in stockpot, add and sauté onions, carrots, garlic, and celery until tender. Add broth and simmer for 15 minutes. Add chayote and simmer for 8 to 10 minutes. Add watercress and simmer 5 more minutes. Chayote should be tender when pierced.

Using a hand-held blender, puree chayote mixture until smooth, season with salt, pepper, and nutmeg.

To serve, ladle into bowls, garnish with tomato strips and watercress.

Approximate Nutrient Content per Serving

Calories	60
Fat	1.5 g
Saturated Fat	0.5 g
Cholesterol	5 mg
Sodium	590 mg
Carbohydrate	9 g
Protein	4 g

This is a soup with character. If using young chayote, the skin is tender and it is not necessary to peel. Seeds are edible and do not need to be removed, but will add fat to the recipe.

Lentil Soup

Hands On: 20 minutes
Unsupervised: 2-1/4 hours

2 cups red lentils

4 cups water

1 tablespoon butter

$\frac{1}{2}$ cup diced onions

$\frac{1}{2}$ cup diced carrots

$\frac{1}{2}$ cup diced celery

2 cloves garlic, minced

1 teaspoon cumin

2 tablespoons tomato
puree

10 cups fat-free, reduced
sodium chicken broth

2 tablespoons sherry

1 teaspoon salt

$\frac{1}{2}$ teaspoon white pepper

$\frac{1}{2}$ cup shredded cooked
turkey breast

2 tablespoons chopped
chives

Presoak lentils in water for 2 hours and drain.

Heat butter in stockpot. Sauté onions, carrots, celery, and garlic until tender. Set aside 1 cup of carrot mixture for later use.

Add cumin and tomato to remaining carrot mixture in pot and sauté for 5 minutes. Add broth and lentils and stir. Simmer until lentils are soft 15 to 20 minutes. Add wine and simmer 5 minutes.

Puree soup with hand-held blender. Season with salt and pepper. Fold into soup the 1 cup of reserved carrot mixture previously set aside.

To serve, ladle soup into individual soup bowls. Garnish with shredded turkey and chives.

**Approximate Nutrient
Content per Serving**

Calories	140
Fat	2 g
Saturated Fat	1 g
Cholesterol	5 mg
Sodium	670 mg
Carbohydrate	20 g
Protein	12 g

Curry powder can be substituted for cumin.

Canadian Bacon, Cauliflower, Cheddar Cheese Soup ♥

Makes 6 Servings

Hands On: 20 minutes
Unsupervised: 10 minutes

2 cups fat-free, reduced sodium chicken broth

2 cups water

3 cups chopped cauliflower florets

1 cup skim milk

1/4 cup cornstarch

1/4 cup tablespoons water

1/3 cup shredded cheddar cheese

1/4 cup julienned Canadian bacon

1/2 teaspoon white pepper

1 teaspoon chopped parsley

Bring broth and water to simmer. Add cauliflower and simmer 5 minutes. Add milk and reduce heat to low, simmer for 5 more minutes.

Mix cornstarch and water together and add to cauliflower-broth mixture. Stir until thickened.

With mixture still at a low simmer, add cheddar cheese and stir until cheese melts. Remove from heat.

Season with white pepper. Ladle into soup bowls, garnish top with Canadian bacon and chopped parsley.

Approximate Nutrient Content per Serving

Calories	80
Fat	2.5 g
Saturated Fat	2 g
Cholesterol	10 mg
Sodium	320 mg
Carbohydrate	10 g
Protein	6 g

This is the low-fat version of our original recipe we used 18 years ago. As you can guess, back then we used butter, whole milk, and heavy cream. Today we appreciate the richness of the flavors of this low-fat version.

Corn and Wild Rice Soup with Smoked Sausage ❤

Makes 8 Servings

Hands On: 25 minute
Unsupervised: 40 minutes

2¹/₂ cups water

¹/₄ cup wild rice

³/₄ cup white wine

3 cups corn kernels

¹/₄ pound smoked turkey sausage

¹/₂ cup diced carrots

¹/₂ cup diced onion

¹/₂ cup diced leek, whites only

¹/₄ cup sliced mushrooms

2¹/₂ cups fat-free, reduced sodium chicken broth

¹/₂ cup skim milk

¹/₄ cup nonfat sour cream

¹/₈ cup chopped chives

¹/₆₄ teaspoon grated nutmeg

Bring water to a boil. Add rice, simmer until liquid evaporates and rice is almost tender. Remove from heat.

Puree 1¹/₂ cups of corn in processor with wine. Set aside.

Cut sausage in half lengthwise and sear all sides in hot skillet. Remove and slice into 1-inch pieces.

In a heavy stock pot, add sausage, carrots, onions, and leeks and sauté for 5 minutes. Add mushrooms and cook for 5 minutes, then add broth and simmer 10 additional minutes.

Add rice and corn puree and remaining corn kernels. Cook until rice is very tender (about15 minutes).

Blend in skim milk and sour cream. Bring back to simmer. Ladle into serving bowls, garnish with chives and barely sprinkle with fresh nutmeg.

Approximate Nutrient Content per Serving

Calories	180
Fat	2 g
Saturated Fat	0.5 g
Cholesterol	15 mg
Sodium	400 mg
Carbohydrate	29 g
Protein	10 g

This soup will bring the kids home for the holidays. The great flavor comes from the leeks and searing the sausage.

Apple and Canadian Bacon Spinach Salad ♥

Makes 4 Servings

Hands On: 20 minutes

$^1/_2$ cup coarsely chopped
Canadian bacon

2 tablespoons fat-free
mayonnaise

1 teaspoon dijon mustard

$^1/_4$ cup apple cider or juice

2 tablespoons balsamic
vinegar*

1 teaspoon chopped garlic

1 teaspoon milled black
pepper*

$^1/_2$ pound fresh spinach
leaves

1 cup diced peeled Granny
Smith apples

Heat frying pan. Add Canadian bacon and cook until bacon is crisp. Remove from pan and place between paper towels to absorb excess oil from bacon.

In a large bowl, combine mayonnaise, mustard, cider, vinegar, garlic, and pepper and whisk until well blended.

Add spinach to bowl with dressing, toss gently. Add apples and fold together.

Divide salad into 4 salad bowls and sprinkle top with bacon. Serve at once.

Approximate Nutrient Content per Serving

Calories	90
Fat	2 g
Saturated Fat	0.5 g
Cholesterol	10 mg
Sodium	410 mg
Carbohydrate	12 g
Protein	6 g

The slight tartness of the Granny Smith apple is important to compliment the other salad ingredients.

Garbanzo Bean and Chicory Salad ❤

1½ cups Walnut Cheese Dressing (next page)

2 medium-sized curly endive*

2 cans (15 ounces) garbanzo beans, rinsed and drained

½ cup diced green bell pepper

1½ cups diced red apples

½ cup grated cooked egg white

3 whole wheat pita pockets

Prepare Walnut Cheese Dressing.

Cut each pita pocket into 8 wedges.

Place chicory leaves on salad plates with the stems of the leaves pointing towards the middle of the plate. Spoon garbanzo beans over leaves and sprinkle with bell peppers, apples, and cooked egg whites.

Drizzle 2 tablespoons of dressing over salad.

Garnish edge of salad with 3 triangles of pita bread.

Approximate Nutrient Content per Serving

Calories	180
Fat	3 g
Saturated Fat	0.5 g
Cholesterol	5 mg
Sodium	270 mg
Carbohydrate	30 g
Protein	10 g

This is a great change to a tossed salad.

Walnut Cheese Dressing

1/2 cup part-skim ricotta
cheese

1 clove garlic

1 tablespoon chopped
chives

3 tablespoons applesauce

1/2 cup plain nonfat yogurt

1/4 teaspoon dry mustard

1/2 cup red wine vinegar

1 tablespoon chopped
walnuts

1/2 teaspoon salt

1/4 teaspoon white pepper

Blend all ingredients in a blender. Pour into small bowl and chill.

**Approximate Nutrient
Content per 2 Tablespoons**

Calories	20
Fat	1 g
Saturated Fat	0 g
Cholesterol	5 mg
Sodium	90 mg
Carbohydrate	2 g
Protein	2 g

The flavor of fresh chives will change after 24 hours, therefore do not refrigerate or store longer than a day.

Mesclun of Greens with Banana Poppyseed Margarita Dressing ♥

Makes 4 Servings

Hands On: 10 minutes

³/₄ cup Banana Poppyseed Margarita Dressing

8 cups mesclun greens*

1 cup plain baked croutons*

Place mesclun greens on salad plates and drizzle 3 tablespoons dressing over salad.

Garnish with croutons and serve.

Approximate Nutrient Content per Serving

Calories	90
Fat	1 g
Saturated Fat	0 g
Cholesterol	0 mg
Sodium	90 mg
Carbohydrate	18 g
Protein	4 g

Mesclun greens are a combination of several different lettuces, some with a strong bite or bitter. The Banana Poppyseed Margarita Dressing compliments each of the lettuces without masking their individuality.

Banana Poppyseed Margarita Dressing

Makes 2$\frac{1}{8}$ cups

Hands On: 5 minutes

$\frac{1}{2}$ cup plain nonfat yogurt

1$\frac{1}{2}$ cups sliced banana

1 teaspoon lemon juice

1 tablespoon honey

1 teaspoon poppyseed

1$\frac{1}{2}$ tablespoons frozen
  concentrate margarita
  mix, thawed

Place all dressing ingredients in blender and blend until smooth. Pour into dressing container. **Refrigerate** until used.

Approximate Nutrient Content per 2 Tablespoons

Calories	30
Fat	0 g
Saturated Fat	0 g
Cholesterol	0 mg
Sodium	5 mg
Carbohydrate	6 g
Protein	1 g

When Chef Al made this dressing, eyebrows were raised with excitement in Fish & Poi Chefs' classes. This dressing accents a simple salad perfectly.

Watercress, Fava Bean and Radicchio Salad ♥

Makes 6 Servings

Hands On: 15 minutes
Unsupervised: 20 minutes

1 cup balsamic vinegar*

2 teaspoons extra virgin olive oil

1/2 cup fat-free, reduced sodium chicken broth

1 pound watercress*

1 1/4 cup radicchio*

2 cups young fresh fava beans*

2/3 cups golden raisins

4 teaspoons grated Parmesan cheese

1/8 teaspoon milled black pepper*

Place vinegar, oil, and broth in bowl and whip. Set bowl into refrigerator until needed.

Wash and drain watercress. Cut and discard lower stems; discard yellow and old leaves. Cut into 1 1/2-inch lengths. Wash and cut radicchio into 1 1/2-inch pieces. Set aside.

Place fresh, raw fava beans into a small pot, cover with water and simmer 3 to 4 minutes. Drain and allow to cool. If fava beans are fully matured, peel the skins off the fava beans. If the beans are young, the skin is tender and does not need peeling.

Soak raisins in hot water for 10 minutes, then drain.

Arrange watercress on salad plate, spoon fava beans on watercress. Sprinkle with raisins. Drizzle with dressing and sprinkle grated cheese over salad and top with black pepper.

Approximate Nutrient Content per Serving

Calories	140
Fat	2 g
Saturated Fat	0.5 g
Cholesterol	0 mg
Sodium	120 mg
Carbohydrate	29 g
Protein	6 g

Dried fava beans could be used, but will not have the same quality of fresh young beans. Prepare the same as any dried bean. Soak overnight and cook.

Side Dishes

In the United States, side dishes are companions to the main course. Often side dishes consist of foods considered as starches or vegetables. In many homes, the same side dishes are served day after day.

We've included a variety of recipes in this section. They include low-fat versions of the old "classics" like fried rice. The majority of the recipes in this section, however, use local ingredients in a new way. We also have included some foods that may be new to you, like quinoa and braised celery. These recipes are simple and can turn a plain meatloaf or roast chicken dinner into a meal to remember.

A good way to assure that we are meeting our nutrient needs is to enjoy eating a wide variety of foods. We hope that these recipes will assist you in adding variety to your diet.

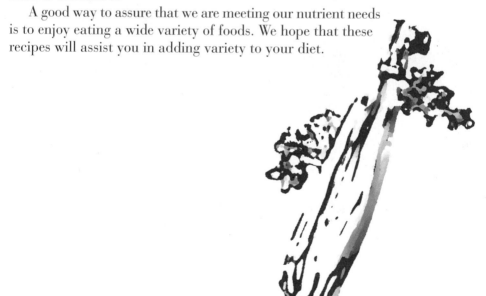

Fried Rice ♥

2 eggs, beaten

5 seconds vegetable oil spray

$\frac{1}{2}$ cup diced onion

$\frac{1}{4}$ cup diced carrots

$\frac{1}{4}$ cup chopped water chestnuts*

4 cups cooked rice, cold

$\frac{1}{4}$ cup reduced sodium soy sauce

$\frac{1}{4}$ cup diced roasted skinless turkey breast

$\frac{2}{3}$ cup diced green onions

In a non-stick pan, cook egg well done. Remove from pan, cool and julienne. Set aside.

Prepare wok with vegetable oil spray. Sauté onions and carrots until tender. Add water chestnuts. Stir in rice until loose and heated thoroughly. Fold in soy sauce and turkey, mix until well heated.

To serve, place rice on 6 dishes and garnish with egg and green onions. Serve hot.

Approximate Nutrient Content per Serving

Calories	190
Fat	3 g
Saturated Fat	0.5 g
Cholesterol	75 mg
Sodium	440 mg
Carbohydrate	32 g
Protein	8 g

Fried rice is a good way to use leftovers. This is a simple version that meets low-fat requirements. Leftover chicken breast can be substituted for the turkey.

Brown Rice Confetti ♥

Makes 6 Servings

Hands On: 5 minutes
Unsupervised: 45 minutes

3 cups water
1/4 teaspoon salt
1 1/2 cups brown rice
1/4 cup diced carrots
1/4 cup diced onion

Rice Cooker Method:

Combine all ingredients. Cover and press "Cook" button. Cooking will take 30 to 40 minutes.

When cooked, fluff rice, cover and allow to sit for 5 minutes before serving.

Stovetop Method:

In a 2-quart sauce pan, bring salt and water to a boil. Add remaining ingredients. Cook for 15 minutes, stirring occasionally until water begins to evaporate and rice begins to puff-up. Replace cover on pot and cook until done (about 30 minutes). Fluff rice and allow to sit 5 minutes before serving.

Approximate Nutrient Content per Serving

Calories	180
Fat	1.5 g
Saturated Fat	0 g
Cholesterol	0 mg
Sodium	100 mg
Carbohydrate	37 g
Protein	4 g

Try adding other chopped vegetables for different flavors.

Risotto* with Shrimp and Radicchio ♥

Makes 6 Servings

Hands On: 25 minutes
Unsupervised: 45 minutes

6 cups water

¹/₂ teaspoon salt

8 cloves garlic, bruised

1 lemon

1 teaspoon olive oil

2 tablespoons chopped shallots

2 cloves garlic, minced

1 cup arborio rice*, rinsed and drained

¹/₂ cup dry white wine

¹/₈ teaspoon white pepper

1 cup cooked shrimp

3 cups thinly sliced radicchio*

2 teaspoons thinly sliced Parmesan cheese

2 teaspoons chopped parsley

In a large stock pot, bring water, salt, bruised garlic, and lemon to a boil. Reduce heat and simmer for 20 minutes. Remove from heat.

Heat oil, sauté shallots and garlic for 2 minutes. Add rice and sauté for 5 minutes. Stir in wine and lower heat to a simmer.

Drain garlic-lemon water into a bowl. Set aside 1 cup of garlic-lemon water to add to shrimp.

Gradually mix into the rice the remaining 5 cups of garlic-lemon water one cup at a time, stirring until liquid nearly evaporates. Rice should be creamy looking and tender.

Add cooked shrimp and radicchio to the rice mixture. Stir in garlic-lemon water previously set-aside. Continue cooking over low heat until liquid is almost evaporated. Risotto should be creamy and smooth.

Approximate Nutrient Content per Serving

Calories	170
Fat	2.5 g
Saturated Fat	1 g
Cholesterol	45 mg
Sodium	32 mg
Carbohydrate	24 g
Protein	9 g

Although somewhat expensive, the combination of the creamy texture of the risotto, the pink tint and sharpness of the radicchio, and the shrimp's refinement makes this dish a perfect treat for a special occasion.

Spanish Rice ♥

Hands On: 15 minutes
Unsupervised: 25 minutes

1 1/2 teaspoons butter

2/3 cup diced onion

2 cloves garlic, minced

3/4 cup long grain rice

2 teaspoons chili powder

1/4 teaspoon cumin

2 tablespoons tomato
   puree

1 bay leaf

1/2 cup diced peeled and
   seeded tomatoes

1 1/2 cup fat-free, reduced
   sodium chicken broth

1/2 cup chopped green bell
   pepper

Heat butter in a sauce pan, add and sauté onions and garlic until tender, (about 3 minutes). Add rice, sauté until rice begins to turn golden beige in color (about 5 minutes).

Add chili powder, cumin, tomato puree, and bay leaf. Stir and sauté for 3 more minutes.

Add tomatoes and stir. Add broth and bring to a boil. Lower heat, partially cover pot, and slowly simmer rice until tender and liquid is absorbed (about 25 minutes).

Fluff rice, and mix in bell peppers. Serve hot.

Approximate Nutrient Content per Serving

Calories	210
Fat	2 g
Saturated Fat	1 g
Cholesterol	5 mg
Sodium	270 mg
Carbohydrate	43 g
Protein	5 g

The secret of this Spanish Rice is patience. Many people add the broth and then all of the spices. By sautéing the spices first, then adding the broth, you allow the spices to "bloom."

Wild Rice Medley ❤

Hands On: 5 minutes
Unsupervised: 30 minutes

5 seconds vegetable oil
spray

¹/₄ cup diced onion

³/₄ cup long grain rice

¹/₄ cup coarse chopped
water chestnuts*

3 cups fat-free, reduced
sodium chicken broth

¹/₄ cup wild rice

¹/₂ cup diced carrots

¹/₂ cup golden raisins

3 tablespoons chopped
green onions

Spray sauté pan lightly with vegetable oil spray. Sauté onions until tender. Add long-grain rice and water chestnuts. Sauté for 5 minutes; set aside.

In a medium size pot, bring broth to a boil. Add wild rice, reduce heat and simmer for 10 minutes uncovered. Then add long rice mixture and carrots. Return to a boil, then cover and simmer undisturbed until rice is tender (about 20 minutes).

Fold raisins and green onions into rice. Serve warm.

**Approximate Nutrient
Content per Serving**

Calories	260
Fat	1.5 g
Saturated Fat	0 g
Cholesterol	0 mg
Sodium	430 mg
Carbohydrate	54 g
Protein	7 g

The small amount of wild rice makes this dish very interesting, yet affordable. When serving a main dish like a roasted Cornish hen, substitute dried apricots for the carrots.

Couscous Molded in Manoa Lettuce ♥

Makes 8 Servings

Hands On: 10 minutes
Unsupervised: 30 minutes

2¹/₂ cups water
¹/₂ teaspoon salt
3 cups couscous*
¹/₂ cup diced carrots
1 strip lemon rind*
¹/₂ cup diced celery
2 cloves garlic, minced
8 large Manoa lettuce*
leaves (or Boston lettuce)
1 - 15-inch square of clean cheese cloth

Combine water and salt. Spread couscous out over a large platter and sprinkle salt water. Gently rub grains with fingertips to separate. Set aside for 15 minutes at room temperature for grains to absorb liquid.

Line perforated top-half of steamer with a dampened piece of cheese cloth. Spread couscous evenly over cheese cloth. Fold excess cloth over couscous. Set aside.

In bottom-half of steamer, bring 2 cups of water to boil. Add carrots, lemon, celery, and garlic; lower heat to simmer. Place covered couscous over vegetables. Simmer for 15 minutes.

Remove top-half of steamer. Blanch lettuce for 2 to 5 seconds, remove and dip in ice water. Drain carrot mixture, discard lemon.

Place couscous in a bowl, fold in carrot mixture.

Line soup cup with lettuce; fill with couscous. Fold excess leaves over top, then unmold onto plates.

Approximate Nutrient Content per Serving

Calories	270
Fat	0 g
Saturated Fat	0 g
Cholesterol	0 mg
Sodium	150 mg
Carbohydrate	55 g
Protein	9 g

Couscous, a native Middle Eastern food, is usually prepared with a stew or braised entrée. The stew is cooked on the bottom half of the steamer, while the couscous is cooked on the top half and absorbs the aroma of the entrée. A bamboo steamer can be used with a wok in place of a steamer.

Mushroom Quinoa ❤

Hands On: 5 minutes
Unsupervised: 15 minutes

6 mushrooms, diced

1/4 cup grated carrots

1/4 cup diced onions

1/4 cup diced celery

2 cups fat-free beef broth

2 cups quinoa*, rinsed and drained

1/4 cup water

In a medium sauce pot, combine mushrooms, carrots, onions, celery, and broth. Bring to a simmer and after 3 minutes, add quinoa. Bring to a boil, then reduce heat and simmer for 12 minutes. Add water if liquid evaporates too soon.

Quinoa is ready when the grain is tender and no liquid remains. Quinoa grains triple in size and kernels begin to pop. It cooks in one half the time of rice.

**Approximate Nutrient
Content per Serving**

Calories	170
Fat	2.5 g
Saturated Fat	0 g
Cholesterol	0 mg
Sodium	55 mg
Carbohydrate	31 g
Protein	7 g

Quinoa was a staple of the Incas. They called it the mother grain. If you want a mild and light side dish to a meal, this is it. Quinoa can be found in health food stores and in some grocery stores.

Lyonnaise Potato ❤

Makes 6 Servings

Hands On: 25 minutes
Unsupervised: 5 minutes

5 cups peeled and sliced russet potatoes (soak potatoes in cold water to prevent browning. Set aside.)

10 seconds butter-flavored oil spray

1 teaspoon salt

1/2 teaspoon white pepper

1 cup sliced onions

1 tablespoon chopped parsley

1 tablespoon chopped green onions

Drain all water from potatoes. Pat dry with a towel.

Evenly coat potatoes with butter-flavored oil spray (5 seconds). In a non-stick pan, heat potatoes on high for 5 to 7 minutes. Stir gently. Season with salt and pepper. Turn potatoes over gently. Cover and turn fire to medium for about 3 minutes.

Spray a second pan with butter-flavored oil spray (5 seconds) and then sauté onions over medium heat until onions are translucent and light brown. Sprinkle over potatoes. When potatoes are cooked, add parsley and green onions. Stir for 1 minute and serve.

Approximate Nutrient Content per Serving

Calories	140
Fat	2 g
Saturated Fat	0 g
Cholesterol	0 mg
Sodium	360 mg
Carbohydrate	29 g
Protein	3 g

The secret to this dish is how the onions are prepared. Slowly sautéing onions until golden brown (caramelizing), produces a sweeter flavor.

Hawaiian Sweet Potato Cakes ❤

Hands On: 25 minutes
Unsupervised: 20 minutes

1 1/2 pounds Okinawan-
 purple sweet potato*

1/4 cup chopped ogo*

1/4 cup diced green onions

1/4 cup julienned
 kamaboko*

1/4 teaspoon hot chili paste*

1/4 cup fat-free egg substitute

1/8 cup mochicho rice flour*

1/2 teaspoon sesame seed
 oil

1/2 teaspoon sesame seeds

6 seconds vegetable oil
 spray

Steam whole potato until cooked (10 to 15 minutes, depending on thickness of potato). The potatoes are cooked when a bamboo skewer can be inserted easily. Remove and chill until cold.

Peel potato and grate into large mixing bowl. Set aside.

In a small bowl, combine remaining ingredients, excluding spray. Whip and blend ingredients with wire whip. Pour mixture over potatoes and evenly fold mixture together.

Lightly spray skillet with vegetable oil spray and heat. Form potato mixture into 4 patties and brown 5 minutes each side. Serve hot.

Approximate Nutrient Content per Serving

Calories	170
Fat	2.5 g
Saturated Fat	0 g
Cholesterol	0 mg
Sodium	150 mg
Carbohydrate	32 g
Protein	5 g

Steam potatoes the day before and chill over night, or use leftover potatoes to prepare this dish in less time. Taro can also be used in place of sweet potatoes, although the final dish will not be as sweet.

Duchess Potato in Tomato Halves ❤

Hands On: 15 minutes
Unsupervised: 20 minutes

3 large tomatoes, halved and seeds removed

2 large russet potatoes

$^1/_4$ teaspoon salt

$^1/_3$ teaspoon white pepper

1 tablespoon chopped parsley

2 teaspoons chopped pimento

$^1/_3$ cup skim milk

Prepare tomatoes, set aside on baking pan.

Peel and dice potatoes. Place in small pot and simmer until potatoes are soft (about 10 minutes). Drain. In a mixing bowl, mash potatoes with a fork. Add salt, pepper, parsley, pimento, and milk, blend until well mixed.

Spoon potato mixture into each tomato.

Place tomatoes on a baking pan and broil for 6 to 7 minutes. Serve hot.

Approximate Nutrient Content per Serving

Calories	60
Fat	0 g
Saturated Fat	0 g
Cholesterol	0 mg
Sodium	105 mg
Carbohydrate	13 g
Protein	2 g

Using a pastry bag with a large fluted tip to pipe the potatoes into the tomatoes will produce a beautiful effect. Please do not use instant mashed potatoes if you want the same quality of "Duchess Potatoes".

Baked Potato Cakes ❤

Makes 6 Servings

Hands On: 15 minutes
Unsupervised: 35 minutes

20 seconds butter-flavored
oil spray

2 pounds thinly sliced
peeled potatoes

¹/₂ teaspoon salt

¹/₂ teaspoon milled black
pepper*

¹/₈ teaspoon nutmeg

2 cloves garlic, minced

1 piece parchment paper
(cut to fit baking dish)

Preheat over to 375 degrees F. Lightly spray bottom of an 8-inch ovenproof dish with butter-flavored oil spray (2 to 3 seconds).

Neatly layer potatoes in a circular pattern on bottom of dish. Lightly spray with vegetable oil spray (2 to 3 seconds) and season potatoes with ¹/₃ of salt, pepper, and nutmeg. Overlap a second and third row of potatoes and season each row as above.

Spray parchment paper with vegetable oil spray (2 to 3 seconds). Cover potatoes with paper. Place potatoes on the bottom rack of a pre-heated oven and bake for 35 minutes.

Remove paper and invert potatoes onto serving dish. Cut into wedges and serve.

**Approximate Nutrient
Content per Serving**

Calories	160
Fat	3 g
Saturated Fat	1.5 g
Cholesterol	5 mg
Sodium	210 mg
Carbohydrate	31 g
Protein	3 g

Do not rinse or put potatoes in water. You want to keep the starch of the potatoes. This will help hold the potatoes together while baking and serving. The thinner the potatoes are cut, the nicer it will look and hold together. Russet potatoes are best.

Grilled Curry Polenta

Makes 6 Servings

Hands On: 25 minutes
Unsupervised: overnight

2 teaspoons butter

$^1/_4$ cup chopped onions

1 tablespoon curry powder

5 cups water

1 teaspoon salt

1 $^1/_2$ cups yellow cornmeal

$^1/_2$ teaspoon salt

$^1/_4$ teaspoon white pepper

Melt 1 teaspoon butter in sauté pan and sauté onions until tender. Add 1 tablespoon curry powder and mix. Remove from heat.

In a heavy sauce pan, bring water and salt to a boil. Gradually add all cornmeal to boiling water. Stirring constantly, cook on low heat until mixture is thick (about 10 minutes). Add remaining teaspoon butter, salt, and white pepper. Add sautéd curried onions. Fold altogether.

Pour batter on baking sheet and evenly spread to sides. Refrigerate overnight.

Cut polenta and warm evenly on a grill. Serve warm.

Approximate Nutrient Content per Serving

Calories	150
Fat	3 g
Saturated Fat	1 g
Cholesterol	5 mg
Sodium	550 mg
Carbohydrate	28 g
Protein	3 g

A non-stick sauté pan can also be used to grill polenta.

Farfalle (Bow-Tie) Pasta with Confetti Vegetables ❤

Makes 8 Servings

Hands On: 20 minutes
Unsupervised: 10 minutes

- 1 pound farfalle pasta
- 2 quarts water
- 3 tablespoons garlic, minced
- 2 cups vegetable broth
- 1/2 cup diced carrots
- 1/4 cup diced celery
- 1/4 cup diced red onion
- 1/2 cup diced zucchini
- 1/4 cup diced yellow squash
- 1/4 cup diced red bell pepper
- 1/4 cup diced green bell pepper

Heat water to a boil in a large pot. Add pasta, stir and simmer until al dente. Remove from heat. Drain, rinse and drain again.

In a large pot, heat vegetable broth to a simmer. Add carrots and simmer for 2 minutes. Then add celery, onion, zucchini, and yellow squash and simmer for 2 minutes. Finally add bell peppers and simmer for 2 minutes. Add pasta and toss gently. Serve hot.

Approximate Nutrient Content per Serving

Calories	250
Fat	1.5 g
Saturated Fat	0 g
Cholesterol	0 mg
Sodium	260 mg
Carbohydrate	50 g
Protein	8 g

Along with hula dancers and musicians, streamers and confetti were often seen as ships sailed from the docks of Hawai'i. This recipe looks good on a plate and brings back memories of those days in Hawai'i.

Thai Rice Noodles ♥

Makes 4 Servings

Hands On: 20 minutes
Unsupervised: 10 minutes

1 teaspoon peanut oil
³/₄ cup julienned carrot
³/₄ cup diced onion
2 cloves garlic, minced
1 inch ginger*, thinly sliced
1 piece lemon grass*, sliced
   diagonally
1 teaspoon minced chili
   pepper
1 tablespoon chopped
   cilantro* stem
¹/₂ cup Vegetable Stock (page
   186)
¹/₂ tablespoons reduced
   sodium soy sauce
8 ounces rice ribbon noodles*
2 tablespoons chopped
   cilantro*
1 tablespoon chopped peanuts
sprigs of Cilantro
2 tablespoons thin sliced mint
   leaves
¹/₄ cup fresh lime juice
1 teaspoon lime zest*

Heat oil, stir-fry carrot, onion, garlic, ginger, lemon grass, chili pepper, and cilantro stems until onion is tender.

Add remaining ingredients in order, stir gently until thoroughly heated (about 8 minutes).

Approximate Nutrient Content per Serving

Calories	260
Fat	2.5 g
Saturated Fat	0 g
Cholesterol	0 mg
Sodium	210 mg
Carbohydrate	51 g
Protein	7 g

This is a great recipe. Easy to make and inexpensive.

Carrot-Zucchini-Squash Wrapped in Spinach ♥

Makes 5 Servings

Hands On: 35 minutes
Unsupervised: 5 minutes

10 large fresh spinach leaves, washed, drained

10 seconds vegetable oil spray

1 cup julienned carrot

1 ½ cup julienned zucchini

1 ½ cup julienned yellow squash

1 cup julienned red bell pepper

1 teaspoon garlic salt

½ teaspoon white pepper

½ cup fat-free, reduced sodium chicken broth

Bring water in sauce pot to a boil. Blanch spinach, drain, chill, and set aside.

Prepare sauté pan with 6 seconds vegetable oil spray. Place carrots in pan, sauté by rolling carrots so they cook evenly and carrots remain facing in the same direction. Remove carrots. Sauté remaining vegetables the same way. When all vegetables are cooked, combine them and roll gently keeping vegetables all facing the same way.

Place 1 spinach leaf on cutting board. Place ⅕ of vegetables on spinach, allowing the tips of vegetables to extend over spinach edge. Roll julienned vegetables with spinach. Place wrapped vegetables over a second spinach leaf and roll so that spinach layer is doubled. Repeat with 4 remaining servings.

Lightly spray sauté pan with vegetable oil spray (4 seconds). Reheat vegetable bundles by gently turning. Add broth and steam 2 minutes. Serve hot.

Approximate Nutrient Content per Serving

Calories	70
Fat	3 g
Saturated Fat	0 g
Cholesterol	15 mg
Sodium	470 mg
Carbohydrate	8 g
Protein	3 g

With a little practice in the art of julienne cutting, you can make this classic and elegant dish.

Steamed Swiss Chard

Makes 4 Servings

Hands On: 5 minutes
Unsupervised: 10 minutes

2 large bunches Swiss chard, cut 1½ inch pieces (about 8 packed cups) Chard reduces to ¼ the volume when cooked so it is important to use this volume of chard.

4 tablespoon grated parmesan cheese

In a steamer, bring water to a boil. Add swiss chard to top of steamer and steam for 8 to 10 minutes.

Remove from steamer, top with grated cheese. Serve hot.

Approximate Nutrient Content per Serving

Calories	70
Fat	2.5 g
Saturated Fat	1.5 g
Cholesterol	5 mg
Sodium	530 mg
Carbohydrate	7 g
Protein	6 g

Children seem to love this dish, even picky eaters. And it's quick.

Baby Bok Choy Oriental

Makes 4 Servings

Hands On: 5 minutes
Unsupervised: 15 minutes

8 whole baby bok choy, washed, drained

¹/₃ cup reduced sodium soy sauce

1 teaspoon sesame seed oil

1 teaspoon toasted sesame seeds

Trim stem end off the bok choy, leaving the bok choy as whole as possible.

Steam bok choy until tender but stem end still crunchy (12 to 15 minutes).

Meanwhile, combine soy sauce, oil and sesame seeds. Place bok choy in large bowl, toss with soy sauce mixture and serve hot.

Approximate Nutrient Content per Serving

Calories	45
Fat	2 g
Saturated Fat	0 g
Cholesterol	0 mg
Sodium	890 mg
Carbohydrate	5 g
Protein	4 g

If fully matured bok choy is available, remove old leaves. Then chop into 2-inch pieces. Prepare as above.

Braised Celery with Roasted Corn and Peppers ♥

Makes 8 Servings

Hands On: 20 minutes
Unsupervised: 25 minutes

1 head of celery, cut into 3-inch lengths

2 cups fat-free, reduced sodium chicken broth

²/₃ cup white wine or ¹/₃ cup white vinegar

1 cup plain low-fat yogurt

1 tablespoon cornstarch

1 tablespoon water

¹/₂ teaspoon salt

¹/₂ teaspoons white pepper

2 cups corn kernels

2 teaspoon canola oil

²/₃ cup diced onion

1 cup diced red bell pepper

Place celery, broth, and wine into sauce pan. Boil for 3 minutes and then simmer for 25 minutes, stirring occasionally.

In a small bowl, combine yogurt, cornstarch, and water. Pour 1 cup of liquid from cooked celery to yogurt mixture and then slowly add yogurt mixture to celery. Gently stir until sauce thickens. Lower heat to barely simmer. Fold in salt and white pepper.

Over medium heat, sauté corn in oil until it begins to brown. Then add onions and sauté until tender. Add red pepper and sauté for 3 additional minutes.

Ladle celery into casserole dish, sprinkle with corn mixture and serve.

Approximate Nutrient Content per Serving

Calories	130
Fat	2.5 g
Saturated Fat	1 g
Cholesterol	5 mg
Sodium	380 mg
Carbohydrate	19 g
Protein	6 g

Braised celery is a typical French dish. This is a low-fat version of a classic.

Lettuce Baked with Creamy Cider ❤

Makes 8 Servings

Hands On: 40 minutes
Unsupervised: 10 minutes

10 seconds vegetable oil spray

1/4 cup diced onions

2 cups peeled apple slices

1 cup apple cider

1 teaspoon salt

6 whole Manoa lettuce* heads

1/2 teaspoon salt

1/2 teaspoon white pepper

1 cup plain non-fat yogurt

2 egg yolks, beaten

1/2 cup fresh bread crumbs

Lightly spray sauté pan with vegetable oil (5 seconds). Sauté onions over medium heat until tender. Add apples and cook 4 minutes. Add cider and simmer for 10 minutes (Apples will turn to a thick puree). Set aside to cool slightly.

Preheat oven to 400 degrees F.

In a large pot, bring salted water to a boil. Submerge lettuce in water and cook for 8 minutes. Remove lettuce, drain well, cool slightly. Roll lettuce into neat rolls and place in a shallow casserole dish.

Season apple puree with salt and pepper. Stir in yogurt and egg. Pour sauce over lettuce and sprinkle with bread crumbs. Spray bread crumbs with vegetable oil spray (5 seconds). Place dish in preheated oven for 10 minutes.

Remove from oven and serve at once.

Approximate Nutrient Content per Serving

Calories	120
Fat	3 g
Saturated Fat	0.5 g
Cholesterol	55 mg
Sodium	350 mg
Carbohydrate	17 g
Protein	7 g

Boston lettuce, radicchio, iceberg, or heart of romaine could be used in place of Manoa lettuce.

Roasted Kabocha Squash ♥

Makes 4 Servings

Hands On: 5 minutes
Unsupervised: 25 minutes

1 1/2 pound kabocha squash*

4 seconds vegetable oil spray

1/4 teaspoon cinnamon

1/8 teaspoon nutmeg

Preheat oven to 350 degree F.

Cut kabocha in half vertically. Remove seeds.

Spray inside of squash lightly with vegetable oil. Sprinkle with cinnamon and nutmeg.

Place cut side down on a baking sheet and bake in middle shelf of oven for 25 minutes.

To serve, cut each half in half and serve hot.

Approximate Nutrient Content per Serving

Calories	40
Fat	1 g
Saturated Fat	0 g
Cholesterol	0 mg
Sodium	0 mg
Carbohydrate	8 g
Protein	1 g

This recipe is simple, adds variety to a meal, and goes well with just about anything.

Candied Butternut Squash Casserole

Makes 4 Servings

Hands On: 15 minutes
Unsupervised: 45 minutes

5 cups diced butternut
  squash

$^1/_4$ cup maple syrup

$^1/_4$ cup vegetable broth

$^1/_2$ cup dried cranberries

$^1/_2$ teaspoon cinnamon

$^1/_4$ teaspoon nutmeg

2 teaspoons soft butter

1 tablespoon lemon juice

1 tablespoon lemon zest*

2 tablespoons chopped
  parsley

2 tablespoons roasted
  pumpkin seeds

Preheat oven to 350 degree F.

In a baking dish, combine all ingredients, except zest, parsley, and pumpkin seeds. Blend together evenly. Cover and bake until squash is tender when pierced with a toothpick (about 45 minutes).

Garnish with lemon zest, parsley and pumpkin seeds. Serve hot.

**Approximate Nutrient
Content per Serving**

Calories	210
Fat	3 g
Saturated Fat	1.5 g
Cholesterol	5 mg
Sodium	105 mg
Carbohydrate	47 g
Protein	2 g

Cranberries make this simple casserole festive and exciting.

Seafood

One of the many joys of living in Hawai'i is easy access to fresh fish and other seafood. From a culinary perspective, seafood has great qualities. The flavors are frequently delicate, blending well with numerous other foods and ingredients. To take full advantage of these flavors, buy fish as fresh as possible. In Hawai'i, this typically means going to the best fish markets early in the morning or asking when fish will be delivered. Better yet, catch your own!

Many people fry their fish. There are many other cooking alternatives that are just as easy and much lower in fat. The options are almost endless: bake, broil, braise, grill, poach, sauté, sear, steam, stew, and stir-fry, to mention a few. Since too much oil can clog the taste buds, much of the natural flavor of the fish is unappreciated when fried.

Seafood requires less time in cooking. Use the cooking times given in the recipes as a guide, but also use your senses to guard against over-cooking.

Ahi Salad with
Champagne Vinaigrette

Makes 2 Servings

Hands On: 40 minutes

¹/₂ cup Champagne Herbal Vinaigrette

1 ¹/₂ cups washed and trimmed curly endive*

12 sliced radicchio* leaves

¹/₄ pound sliced watercress*

¹/₂ cup thinly sliced red onion

6 ounces fresh ahi* (cut 4 x 2 x 1-inch)

1 teaspoon salt

2 teaspoons chopped shallots

2 cloves chopped garlic

1 tablespoon chopped fresh basil

1 tablespoon cracked pepper

5 seconds vegetable oil spray

1 cup shredded carrots

1 cup shredded daikon*

¹/₂ tablespoon enoki* mushrooms

Approximate Nutrient Content per Serving

Calories	230
Fat	4 g
Saturated Fat	0 g
Cholesterol	40 mg
Sodium	1250 mg
Carbohydrate	23 g
Protein	25 g

Mix endive, radicchio, watercress, and red onion. Toss lightly until evenly mixed. Keep chilled in refrigerator.

Over a plate, sprinkle ahi with salt, shallots, garlic, basil, and cracked pepper. Press ahi gently to ensure all spices and herbs stick to ahi.

Spray vegetable oil on a sauté pan. When heat is high, cook ahi for about 4 minutes on each side. Remove from pan and cool for 3 minutes. Slice into thin slices and set aside.

To serve, place a handful of salad in the center of a large entree plate. Divide sliced ahi in two and arrange slices around plate rim with spaces in between ahi.

Garnish center of salad with shredded carrots and daikon. Along sides of each piece of ahi, place some enoki mushrooms.

Drizzle ¹/₈ cup vinaigrette over each salad. Serve immediately.

Champagne Herbal Vinaigrette

Makes 1 ½ cups

Hands On: 10 minutes

⅛ teaspoon fresh thyme leaves

⅛ teaspoon marjoram

⅛ teaspoon tarragon leaves

⅛ teaspoon oregano leaves

½ teaspoon chopped fresh basil

1 teaspoon minced parsley

½ cup red wine vinegar

1 tablespoon Worcestershire sauce

1 tablespoon sugar

1/16 teaspoon Tabasco®

½ cup fat-free, reduced sodium chicken broth

½ cup champagne vinegar or champagne

1 teaspoon lemon juice

1 teaspoon lime juice

Combine all ingredients in a blender for 1 minute.

Refrigerate.

Approximate Nutrient Content per 2 Tablespoons

Calories	20
Fat	0 g
Saturated Fat	0 g
Cholesterol	0 mg
Sodium	40 mg
Carbohydrate	2 g
Protein	0 g

This is a dressing that is excellent with nearly any salad or as a marinade for chicken or fish.

Curried Monchong in Rice Wrappers with Cucumber Tomato Relish ♥ Makes 4 Servings

Hands On: 15 minutes
Unsupervised: 70 minutes

³/₄ cup Cucumber Tomato
   Relish (next page)

2 tablespoons lime juice

2 tablespoons lime zest*

1¹/₂ teaspoon chili oil*

2 tablespoons soy sauce

3 tablespoons minced lemon
   grass*

2 tablespoons curry powder

2 tablespoons grated ginger*

2 cloves garlic, minced

¹/₂ teaspoon cumin powder

4 monchong* fillets
   (4 ounces each)

4 sheets dried rice paper*
   (8-inch diameter)

4 thin slices lime

4 sprigs cilantro*

3 seconds vegetable oil spray

Prepare Cucumber Tomato Relish.

Mix juice, zest, oil, soy sauce, lemon grass, curry, ginger, garlic, and cumin. Blend well, then roll fish in marinade and allow to marinate at least 1 hour.

Preheat oven to 350 degrees F.

Dampen rice wrappers. In the center of each wrapper, place lime slice, cilantro, and then fish. Fold ends of wrapper over fish. Repeat 3 times.

Lightly spray skillet with vegetable oil spray. Bring heat to medium and quickly sear both sides of the wrapped fish. Place wrapped fish on baking pan and bake for 7 minutes.

Top each warm wrapper with ¹/₄ cup Tomato Cucumber Relish.

**Approximate Nutrient
Content per Serving**

Calories	220
Fat	6 g
Saturated Fat	1 g
Cholesterol	40 mg
Sodium	560 mg
Carbohydrate	16 g
Protein	26 g

Great presentation and great flavors.

Cucumber Tomato Relish

Makes 1³/₄ cups

Hands On: 15 minutes

1 teaspoon olive oil

¹/₂ teaspoon chili oil*

¹/₂ teaspoon sesame seed
   oil

1 1-inch piece ginger*,
   grated

1 teaspoon minced garlic

1 cup peeled and seeded
   diced cucumber

1 cup diced plum tomatoes

¹/₄ teaspoon soy sauce

¹/₈ teaspoon white pepper

¹/₈ teaspoon sugar

¹/₈ teaspoon toasted
   sesame seeds

Combine all ingredients into heated skillet. Sauté for 4 to 5 minutes. Set aside. Serve at room temperature. If refrigerated, reheat before serving.

**Approximate Nutrient
Content per 2 Tablespoons**

Calories	10
Fat	0.5 g
Saturated Fat	0 g
Cholesterol	0 mg
Sodium	5 mg
Carbohydrate	1 g
Protein	0 g

Grating the ginger, rather than chopping, is important to achieve the right flavors.

Opah with Orange Mustard Glaze ♥

Makes 5 Servings

Hands On: 10 minutes
Unsupervised: 10 minutes

½ cup orange juice

1 tablespoon orange zest*

2 tablespoons lime juice

1 teaspoon lime zest*

2 tablespoons brown sugar

¼ cup prepared brown mustard

1 teaspoon dry English mustard

1 cup chopped onions

1 cup sliced green bell peppers

1 cup mung bean sprouts*

5 pieces opah* (5 ounces each)

3 seconds vegetable oil spray

In a small sauce pan, heat juices, zests, brown sugar, and mustards. Stir sauce until sugar dissolves (about 1 minute). Remove glaze from heat and set aside.

Set oven on broil.

Mix onions and peppers. Steam briefly (about 5 minutes) and add bean sprouts. Stir and set aside.

Prepare broiler pan with vegetable oil spray. Place outside flesh of fish side down on broiler pan, brush with glaze. Place in oven and broil for 2 to 3 minutes (depending on thickness).

Turn fish over, brush with glaze and broil second side until fish is done (about 2 minutes).

Place fish on plate with mixed steamed vegetables and brush with glaze. Serve hot.

Approximate Nutrient Content per Serving

Calories	190
Fat	6 g
Saturated Fat	1.5 g
Cholesterol	40 mg
Sodium	250 mg
Carbohydrate	14 g
Protein	21 g

The oven broiler is really easy to use. But if you prefer, heat a non-stick skillet over medium-high heat, place fish into skillet and brush glaze on top of fish. Cook for 2 to 3 minutes. Turn fish over, brush with glaze and cook for 2 to 3 more minutes.

Opakapaka* Florentine

Makes 6 Servings

Hands On: 10 minutes
Unsupervised: 15 minutes

20 ounces chopped frozen spinach, thawed

1 cup part-skim ricotta cheese

1 tablespoon grated parmesan cheese

$1/_2$ cup fat-free egg substitute

$1/_2$ cup minced onion

2 tablespoons chopped fresh basil

$1/_2$ teaspoon white pepper

4 cloves garlic, minced

6 opakapaka* fillets (3 ounces each), cut $1/_4$-inch thick

1 cup non-alcoholic wine

Preheat oven to 375 degrees F.

Place spinach in a strainer, press out the excess liquid.

In a medium bowl, combine spinach, ricotta cheese, parmesan, egg substitute, onion, basil, pepper, and garlic. Mix well.

Spread spinach mixture on top of each fillet, roll-up, insert toothpick to hold together. Place rolls in a baking dish, add non-alcoholic wine. Cover with lid or parchment paper.

Bake for 10 to 15 minutes, depending on thickness of fish.

Remove toothpicks, slice and serve hot.

Approximate Nutrient Content per Serving

Calories	190
Fat	5 g
Saturated Fat	2.5 g
Cholesterol	45 mg
Sodium	230 mg
Carbohydrate	9 g
Protein	28 g

This pink snapper recipe is easy to prepare and tastes like it took hours.

Poached Uku with Papaya Relish ❤

Makes 4 Servings

Hands On: 15 minutes
Unsupervised: 10 minutes

Papaya* Relish (next page)

1 quart Fish Stock (page 188)

4 uku* fillets (5-ounces each)

4 ti leaves*

4 lime twists

Prepare Papaya Relish.

In a sauce pan, bring fish stock to a boil, then lower heat to simmer. Gently place fish into stock and simmer for 7 minutes. Remove fish with slotted flat spoon.

To serve, place ti leaf on plate, angle fish crisscross over ti leaf, lace 1 tablespoon papaya relish across fish. Garnish with lime. Serve hot.

Approximate Nutrient Content per Serving

Calories	200
Fat	2.5 g
Saturated Fat	0.5 g
Cholesterol	65 mg
Sodium	80 mg
Carbohydrate	4 g
Protein	37 g

To make this easier, fat-free, reduced sodium chicken broth can be substituted for fish stock. The sodium content will increase slightly.

Papaya Relish ❤

I tablespoon lime juice

I cup diced papaya*

2 tablespoons minced red
onion

2 tablespoons minced
green onion

I teaspoon grated ginger*

I tablespoon brandy

I tablespoon honey

Combine all ingredients for relish, mix well. Refrigerate until needed.

**Approximate Nutrient
Content per 2 Tablespoons**

Calories	20
Fat	0 g
Saturated Fat	0 g
Cholesterol	0 mg
Sodium	0 mg
Carbohydrate	4 g
Protein	0 g

Red wine vinegar can be used in place of brandy.

Poached Whole Onaga with Wine, Caper, and Tomato Sauce ❤

Makes 4 Servings

Hands On: 15 minutes
Unsupervised: 30 minutes

2 pound fresh whole onaga*, scaled, and cleaned

2 quart Fish Stock (page 188)

1 cup dry white wine

2 bunches parsley stems

2 bay leaves

2 tablespoons capers*

2 tablespoons cornstarch

2 tablespoons water

1 cup peeled, seeded and diced tomatoes

8 thin, round lemon slices

2 tablespoon capers*

1 tablespoon chopped parsley

Preheat oven 375 degrees F.

Rinse fish and be sure it is gutted cleanly. Set aside.

In a fish poaching pan (large enough to hold fish), combine stock, wine, parsley stems, bay leaves, and capers. Bring to a boil for 10 minutes over stove. Lower heat. Gently place whole fish into liquid, cover and place in oven. Check for doneness at 12, 17, and 20 minutes.

With 2 long spatulas supporting the fish, remove and set it on a serving platter. Take 1½ cups of fish liquid, bring it to a boil over the stove. Mix cornstarch and water, add to liquid. Add tomato and simmer for 2 minutes.

To serve, ladle sauce over fish. Layer lemon slices down fish, sprinkle with capers and parsley. Serve hot.

Approximate Nutrient Content per Serving

Calories	200
Fat	2 g
Saturated Fat	0 g
Cholesterol	50 mg
Sodium	280 mg
Carbohydrate	8 g
Protein	29 g

To determine when a fish is cooked, check the eye. When raw, the eye is set in the eye socket. With cooking, the eye turns opaque, becomes firm and emerges from the eye socket. When cooked, the eye looks like a small marble and ¾ emerged from the socket. If it has fallen out, the fish is over cooked.

Grilled Ahi with Miso Glaze and Grilled Vegetables ❤

Makes 4 Servings

Hands On: 15 minutes
Unsupervised: 60 minutes

2 tablespoons lime juice

1 tablespoon lime zest*

1 tablespoon grated
ginger*

1/4 cup sake* or mirin*

1/4 teaspoon hot chili paste*

2 tablespoons red miso*

4 ahi* steaks (5 ounces
each), 1/2-inch thick

2 medium zucchini

2 medium long eggplant

2 medium yellow zucchini

3 seconds vegetable oil
spray

2 cups finely shredded
cabbage

4 lime wedges

1 tablespoon slivered green
onions

1 teaspoon furikake*

Approximate Nutrient Content per Serving

Calories	240
Fat	3 g
Saturated Fat	0.5 g
Cholesterol	65 mg
Sodium	400 mg
Carbohydrate	13 g
Protein	37 g

Combine and mix all juice, zest, ginger, sake, chili paste, and miso. Roll fish gently in sauce, covering evenly. Place fish in a single layer and refrigerate for at least 1 hour.

Cut zucchini lengthwise in half and then in half again forming 4 wedges. Repeat with eggplant and yellow zucchini (Do not trim ends of vegetables). Lay vegetables flat on cutting board and lightly coat with vegetable oil spray.

Start charcoal grill. Make sure grill rack is clean, spray vegetable oil spray lightly on rack and then place over charcoal to heat. Place vegetables on grill at an angle to gain even grill marks. Broil 2 minutes and turn for 2 more minutes. (Do not move while grilling). Remove vegetables to cutting board.

Grill fish same as vegetables, 4 minutes each side. Meanwhile, cut each vegetable 3-inch lengths. Layer vegetables in an alternating pattern forming a ring. Place 1/2 cup cabbage in center of vegetables. Place grilled ahi over cabbage and garnish with lime wedges, green onions and furikake.

Grilled foods are always eye-appealing. Marinating adds flavor.

Striped Sea Bass Steamed in Chinese Tradition

Makes 6 Servings

Hands On: 10 minutes
Unsupervised: 20 minutes

2 pounds fresh striped sea bass, scaled and internal organs removed

2 large ti leaves

1 tablespoon chopped ginger*

3 tablespoons reduced sodium soy sauce

$^{1}/_{2}$ tablespoons sugar

2 cloves garlic, minced

2 tablespoons rice wine*

2 cups fat-free, reduced sodium chicken broth

1 cup thinly sliced shiitake mushrooms*

1 cup sliced green onions

$^{1}/_{2}$ cup thinly sliced omelet from fat-free egg substitute

On both sides of fish, score diagonal cuts at a slight angle through flesh about 1 to 2-inches apart. Set fish into ti leaf and place in shallow steamer.

Combine ginger, soy sauce, sugar, garlic, rice wine, and broth. Blend well and pour over fish. Cover fish with shiitake, then green onions and egg slices. Cover fish with ti leaf.

Cover steamer with lid and steam for 20 minutes. Once or twice baste sauce over fish. Check eye for doneness (see page 86 for tip).

Discard ti leaf. Gently transfer fish to large serving platter and arrange shiitake mushrooms, green onions, and omelet on top of fish.

Approximate Nutrient Content per Serving

Calories	170
Fat	3 g
Saturated Fat	0.5 g
Cholesterol	95 mg
Sodium	640 mg
Carbohydrate	7 g
Protein	26 g

This recipe was originated by Raymond Chu (Chef Pat's dad). An acceptable ingredient substitution for chicken broth in this recipe is Fish Stock (page 188). This will lower the sodium content. Always be cautious of bones when eating fish.

Nairagi Baked with Ricotta Cheese and Apple Banana

Makes 6 Servings

Hands On: 15 minutes
Unsupervised: 20 minutes

2 seconds vegetable oil spray

$^1/_4$ cup minced onions

$^1/_4$ cup minced mushrooms

1 tablespoon minced lemon grass*

1 tablespoon minced cilantro*

$^2/_3$ cup dry white wine

2 tablespoons Roasted Garlic Paste (page 194)

1 teaspoon ginger juice*

$^1/_2$ cup part-skim ricotta cheese

2 diced apple banana*

$^1/_2$ cup fresh bread crumbs

1 can (10 ounces) diced tomatoes

6 nairagi* fillets sliced $^1/_2$-inch thick (5-ounces each)

1 teaspoon salt

$^1/_2$ teaspoon black pepper

$^1/_2$ teaspoon paprika

Approximate Nutrient Content per Serving

Calories	280
Fat	8 g
Saturated Fat	2.5 g
Cholesterol	60 mg
Sodium	610 mg
Carbohydrate	13 g
Protein	32 g

Preheat oven to 375 degrees F.

Spray sauté pan with vegetable oil spray. Sauté onions, mushrooms, and lemon grass until tender. Add cilantro, sauté for 2 minutes, then add wine, garlic paste, and ginger juice. Sauté until $^3/_4$ of wine evaporates. Remove from heat and cool.

In a food processor, puree cheese and bananas. Add bread crumbs and blend evenly. Add half of onion mixture and blend together. Add the tomatoes and liquid to the remaining onion mixture in the sauté pan. Return sauté pan to low heat and simmer until mixture thickens (12 to 15 minutes).

With a de-boning knife, cut a small horizontal pocket into the center of the fillet, without cutting through surrounding edges of fillet. Fill fillet pocket with cheese mixture. Place fish on baking sheet, season with salt, pepper, and paprika. Place in oven and bake for about 15 minutes.

To serve, place fish fillet on plate and ladle tomato sauce over fish. Serve hot.

A teaspoon of minced garlic can be used in place of roasted garlic paste.

Caramelized Halibut with Honey Dijon Cucumber Yogurt ♥

Makes 4 Servings

Hands On: 10 minutes
Unsupervised: 15 minutes

1 cup Honey Dijon Cucumber Yogurt (Next page)

4 halibut steaks (6 ounces) $\frac{1}{2}$-inch thick

3 tablespoons sugar

3 seconds vegetable oil spray

2 tablespoons soy sauce

8 chive stems

Prepare Honey Dijon Cucumber Yogurt.
Preheat oven to 350 degrees F.
With paper towel, pat dry halibut. Sprinkle sugar evenly onto a platter. Lay only one side of fish in sugar.

Lightly spray sauté pan. Heat pan to medium high. Place sugar side of fish on surface of sauté pan. Do not move fish around, rather allow it to sear and caramelize (3 to 4 minutes).

Turn fish over and pour soy sauce over fish and bottom of pan. Sear second side 3 minutes. Remove fish to baking sheet and place with sugar side up.

Bake 8 to 12 minutes. Fish will finish cooking and caramelizing in oven.

To serve, place fish on plate, drizzle $\frac{1}{4}$ cup of Honey Dijon Cucumber Yogurt across fish and criss-cross chives over fish. Serve warm.

Approximate Nutrient Content per Serving

Calories	270
Fat	5 g
Saturated Fat	0.5 g
Cholesterol	55 mg
Sodium	600 mg
Carbohydrate	15 g
Protein	39 g

Pan must be clean prior to caramelizing fish in order to prevent an undesirable burnt taste.

Honey Dijon Cucumber Yogurt

Makes 1³/₄ cups

Hands On: 10 minutes

1 cup plain nonfat yogurt

1 tablespoon lime juice

¹/₂ teaspoon lime zest*

2 teaspoons honey

1 teaspoon dijon mustard

¹/₂ cup minced peeled and
    seeded cucumber

¹/₈ teaspoon white pepper

¹/₄ cup minced tomato
    peeled and seeded

Combine nonfat yogurt, lime juice, lime zest, honey, Dijon mustard, cucumber, and white pepper. Mix well.

Gently fold in tomato.

Refrigerate and use within two days.

**Approximate Nutrient
Content per 2 Tablespoons**

Calories	15
Fat	0 g
Saturated Fat	0 g
Cholesterol	0 mg
Sodium	25 mg
Carbohydrate	3 g
Protein	1 g

This recipe can be used with all types of other dishes, such as a fresh vegetable dip or substitute for tartar sauce.

Shutome Made Easy

Makes 5 Servings

Hands On: 5 minutes
Unsupervised: 15 minutes

1 cup nonfat dark red French dressing

1 package onion soup mix

1 cup crushed pineapple*

1 tablespoon light golden brown sugar

5 shutome* fillets (5-ounces each), $1/_2$-inch thick

$3^1/_3$ cups cooked brown rice

Preheat oven to 350 degrees F.

In a sauce pan, combine French dressing, onion soup mix, pineapple, and sugar. Heat until soup mix and sugar dissolve. Remove from heat.

Pour sauce in a large baking dish. Roll fish in sauce and then place fish side-by-side. Bake uncovered for 15 minutes. Remove from oven.

Scoop $2/_3$ cup hot brown rice in center of plate and flatten with spoon forming a bed. Place fillet and sauce over rice.

Approximate Nutrient Content per Serving

Calories	430
Fat	7 g
Saturated Fat	2 g
Cholesterol	55 mg
Sodium	1100 mg
Carbohydrate	55 g
Protein	31 g

This is one of Katherine Chu's (Chef Pat's mom) quick and easy recipes. It can also be done the same way with other firm, mild tasting fish or even with chicken.

Fresh Water Prawn and Seared Scallops with Star Fruit and Saffron Cream

Makes 2 Servings

Hands On: 15 minutes
Unsupervised: 20 minutes

6 whole fresh water
prawns, 3 to 4-inches
long

2 tablespoons dry white
wine

1 teaspoon ginger juice*

1 teaspoon sugar

1 teaspoon minced
cilantro* stems

$1/2$ teaspoon white pepper

8 large scallops

6 slices star fruit (from the
smallest end of fruit)

$1/2$ cup Star Fruit and
Saffron Cream (next
page)

2 seconds vegetable oil
spray

Cilantro sprigs

Trim prawns feelers and legs. Cut a shallow incision down the back, but do not cut completely through. Blend wine, juice, sugar, cilantro, and pepper. Marinade prawns, scallops, and star fruit slices for 20 minutes.

Prepare Star Fruit and Saffron Cream.

Lightly spray a sauté pan with vegetable oil spray. Heat and sear scallops, prawns, and star fruit for 2 to 3 minutes on each side. Do not over cook. Leave in pan and remove from heat.

To serve, overlap 3 seared star fruit at top of each plate, ladle 3 tablespoons sauce in center of plate. Lay prawns across star fruit and cascade scallops from the star fruit to the sauce. Garnish with cilantro.

**Approximate Nutrient
Content per Serving**

Calories	300
Fat	4 g
Saturated Fat	0.5 g
Cholesterol	285 mg
Sodium	410 mg
Carbohydrate	10 g
Protein	48 g

Star Fruit is in season May and June, then again in November and December.

Star Fruit and Saffron Cream

Makes 1 ½ cups

Hands On: 10 minutes
Unsupervised: 15 minutes

4 seconds vegetable oil spray

2 tablespoons chopped shallots

1 teaspoon minced garlic

1 teaspoon minced ginger*

½ cup white wine

½ cup fat-free, reduced sodium chicken broth

⅔ cup chopped star fruit*

¼ teaspoon saffron threads

Lightly spray a sauté pot, heat pot and sauté shallots and garlic until tender. Add ginger. Sauté 3 more minutes. Add white wine, broth, and star fruit. Bring to a boil for 4 minutes, then simmer for 10 minutes.

With a hand held blender, puree sauce mixture until smooth.

Fold saffron into sauce and allow to simmer for 3 minutes.

Approximate Nutrient Content per 2 Tablespoons

Calories	15
Fat	0 g
Saturated Fat	0 g
Cholesterol	0 mg
Sodium	20 mg
Carbohydrate	1 g
Protein	0 g

This is a great way to enjoy star fruit other than in a salad or eating it by itself.

Squid Simmered In Asian-Mediterranean Flavors

Makes 5 Servings

Hands On: 15 minutes
Unsupervised: 10 minutes

1½ pounds cleaned squid tubes and tentacles (squid body 2 to 3-inches long)

2 seconds vegetable oil spray

½ cup diced onions

¼ cup Roasted Garlic Paste (page 194)

½ teaspoon hot chili paste*

1 can (28 ounces) plum tomatoes

1 cup clam juice

1 cup mirin*

1 stalk lemon grass*, minced

5 thinly sliced basil leaves

¼ cup julienned yellow bell pepper for garnish

Split squid tubes in half lengthwise. With a knife, lightly score tubes diagonally ¼-inch, then lightly score in opposite direction diagonally to create a crosshatch pattern. Be careful to cut only half way through squid. Set aside.

Prepare sauté pan with vegetable oil spray and sauté onions until golden in color.

In a food processor, puree garlic paste, chili paste, and tomatoes until smooth.

In a medium sauce pot, combine tomato mixture, clam juice, mirin, and lemon grass. Bring to a boil for 2 minutes, then lower heat and simmer for 10 minutes. Add squid tubes, tentacles and basil. Simmer covered for 2 minutes. (Squid cooks very quickly, especially if scored. Overcooking will make squid rubbery and tough). Remove from heat.

To serve, ladle squid into individual casserole bowls and garnish with peppers.

Approximate Nutrient Content per Serving

Calories	310
Fat	3 g
Saturated Fat	0.5 g
Cholesterol	320 mg
Sodium	440 mg
Carbohydrate	34 g
Protein	25 g

Roasted garlic paste gives an entirely different flavor to this dish than raw garlic. This paste is somewhat sweeter and smoother than cooking with raw garlic. Sake or rice vinegar* can be used in place of mirin.*

Shellfish Bourride*

Hands On: 15 minutes
Unsupervised: 25 minutes

1 quart Shellfish Stock
(next page)

5 slices French bread,
$1/_4$-inch thick

15 Manila clams, washed

5 mussels, washed

10 scallops

10 shrimps (about $1/_2$
pound)

5 crab claws

$1/_2$ cup Roasted Garlic Paste
(page 194)

$1/_2$ cup fat-free mayonnaise

2 teaspoons orange zest*

2 teaspoons chopped
parsley

Prepare Shellfish stock.

Preheat oven to 325 degrees F. Place French bread slices on baking sheet and place in preheated oven until even golden brown. Turn slices over to brown other side. Remove from oven and cool.

To Shellfish Stock, add lobster, clams, mussels, scallops, and crab and simmer for 5 minutes. Place toast in the middle of large shallow soup bowls. Divide shellfish from stock evenly into bowls. Return stock to heat and simmer.

In a bowl, combine garlic paste with mayonnaise. Add $1/_3$ cup stock and blend with garlic-mayonnaise paste. Then slowly drizzle mayonnaise mixture into stock, while constantly whipping stock. Ladle liquid into bowls with shellfish. Garnish with zest and parsley and serve immediately.

Approximate Nutrient Content per Serving

Calories	550
Fat	4 g
Saturated Fat	1 g
Cholesterol	160 mg
Sodium	1230 mg
Carbohydrate	36 g
Protein	49 g

Chef Pat became acquainted with a very well-traveled elderly guest. For two months she asked Chef Pat to make various meals she had savored in her travels. Bourride was from Nice, France. This low-fat version, using only shellfish, resembles the fullness of flavor as the original. It is similar to bouillabaisse, but bourride has a character of its own.

Shellfish Stock

Hands On: 15 minutes
Unsupervised: 1 hour

I spiny lobster tail
(10 ounces)

7 cups water

5 cups dry white wine

1 1/2 cup diced leeks, white
part only

3/4 cup diced onion

1/2 cup diced carrots

1/4 teaspoon saffron threads

2 cloves garlic, chopped

I tablespoon orange zest*

2 tablespoons frozen
orange juice concen-
trate, thawed

2 bay leaves

1/2 teaspoon milled black
pepper*

Remove lobster from shell and use shell for stock and reserve lobster for bourride. Cut lobster into 5 even pieces and refrigerate until needed.

Into a 4-quart stockpot, combine all ingredients, including lobster shell. Bring to a boil for 5 minutes, lower heat and simmer for 20 minutes.

Strain stock into 2 quart stockpot, discard shell and vegetables. Bring strained stock to a boil, lower heat to simmer, and reduce to 1 quart of liquid.

**Approximate Nutrient
Content per Cup**

Calories	210
Fat	1.5 g
Saturated Fat	0 g
Cholesterol	0 mg
Sodium	25 mg
Carbohydrate	5 g
Protein	1 g

Save raw shrimp and lobster shells in the freezer to add flavor to stocks and sauces.

Buckwheat Soba
Sea of Japan

Makes 4 Servings

Hands On: 20 minutes
Unsupervised: 15 minutes

2 quarts water

1 piece dried cuttlefish*

1 piece dried kombu*

1 tablespoon bonito flakes*

1 teaspoon dashi*

1 tablespoon mirin*

12 ounces dried soba*

1 tablespoon Yamasa® light
(in color) soy sauce

1/2 cup sliced steamed
carrots

1/2 cup chopped won bok*

1/2 cup mung bean sprouts*

1/2 cup spinach

1/2 cup sliced shiitake
mushrooms*

1/4 cup julienned cooked
fat-free egg substitute

4 thin slices kamaboko*

2 tablespoons chopped
green onions

Approximate Nutrient Content per Serving

Calories	370
Fat	1 g
Saturated Fat	0 g
Cholesterol	15 mg
Sodium	1250 mg
Carbohydrate	79 g
Protein	19 g

In a stockpot, bring water, cuttlefish, kombu, bonito, dashi, and mirin to boil for 5 minutes. Cover. Remove from heat and allow to steep for 10 minutes with everything left inside.

While the cuttlefish broth is steeping, put all sliced vegetables into bamboo steamer and steam for 10 minutes.

In another pot, bring 1 quart water to boil, add soba, stir gently and cook for 4 minutes and drain.

To assemble: Bring broth to a rapid boil. Strain broth into 2 large saimin bowls. Divide soba into 2 bowls, drizzle 1 1/2 tablespoon soy sauce in each bowl. Divide carrots, won bok, bean sprouts, spinach, shiitake mushrooms, egg, kamaboko, and green onions. Serve hot.

The cuttlefish gives unique flavor to this broth.

Stir-Fried Shrimp with Peking Sauce ♥

Makes 4 Servings

Hands On: 15 minutes
Unsupervised: 5 minutes

3 seconds vegetable oil spray

2 cloves garlic, chopped

2 slices ginger*

3 cups chopped mustard cabbage

1 cup fat-free, reduced sodium chicken broth

2 teaspoons light (in color) soy sauce

1 teaspoon oyster sauce*

1 pound shrimp, peeled and deveined

1 tablespoon water

1 tablespoon cornstarch

Lightly spray wok with vegetable oil spray. Heat and stir fry garlic and ginger for 30 seconds.

Add cabbage and stir fry for 2 minutes. Add broth, soy sauce, oyster sauce, and simmer. Stir well. Add shrimp and cook evenly.

Combine water and cornstarch. Add to wok. Cook for 2 -3 minutes until sauce thickens and coats shrimp and vegetables. Serve immediately.

Approximate Nutrient Content per Serving

Calories	150
Fat	3 g
Saturated Fat	0 g
Cholesterol	150 mg
Sodium	580 mg
Carbohydrate	8 g
Protein	22 g

Quick and easy! If mustard cabbage is too strong for your taste, use a milder cabbage like Chinese cabbage.

Lobster with Wine and Saffron Sauce

Makes 2 Servings

Hands On: 15 minutes
Unsupervised: 35 minutes

2 spiny lobster tails
(6 ounces each)

2 cups water

1 lemon cut in half

$^1/_4$ cup dry white wine

1 $^1/_2$ teaspoon cornstarch

$^1/_3$ cup evaporated skim milk

1/8 teaspoon saffron threads

1 teaspoon lime juice

$^1/_4$ teaspoon white pepper

1 teaspoon soft butter

1 teaspoon lime zest*

With kitchen shears, gently cut both underneath edges of the lobster shell. Do not cut the meat. Leave the tail fins, the last shell segment connected to the fin and lobster meat attached. Save lobster shell. Insert a bamboo skewer through center of lobster meat, refrigerate until needed.

Place lobster shells, and water into stockpot, squeeze and drop lemon into liquid. Bring to boil, then simmer for 15 minutes.

Meanwhile, prepare sauce by simmering wine in sauce pan for 5 minutes. Whisk milk and cornstarch together and whisk into wine. Allow to thicken and simmer for 10 minutes. Add saffron, lime juice, and pepper. Simmer 10 minutes, stirring occasionally.

Remove lobster shells from stock. Place lobster meat in simmering stock. Cook lobster until firm (8 to 10 minutes). Remove from stock. Remove skewer and slice lobster into medallions. Fan medallions on plate with tail-fin fanned out.

Whisk butter into sauce. Ladle sauce only over meat, not on fin or shell. Garnish with lime zest. Serve hot.

Approximate Nutrient Content per Serving

Calories	270
Fat	4.5 g
Saturated Fat	1.5 g
Cholesterol	125 mg
Sodium	370 mg
Carbohydrate	11 g
Protein	38 g

For a special occasion, this is a perfect meal. This is a recipe that turns you into a pro.

Poultry

Poultry is an important ingredient in the cuisine of many cultures. Chicken is especially universal with many more chicken recipes around the world than cultures. Some of the standards include: chicken stir-fry, chicken yakitori, chicken piccata, chicken long rice, chicken Véronique, chicken fajitas, chicken kal-bi and many chicken curries, to name a few.

Poultry lends itself to lower fat cooking by removing the skin (and much of the fat beneath it) and using the lower fat white meat in poultry breast. These changes can easily convert high-fat recipes into low-fat or reduced fat versions.

As with all food purchasing and preparation, it is important that the food be safe. When purchasing poultry, make sure that the bird has no dark blemishes or strong odors. If you have frozen chicken or turkey, thaw it in the refrigerator. Keep chicken chilled until ready to cook. Meat should be cooked evenly throughout, especially if there is a bone. Meat should not look pink or raw.

Szechuan Chicken Skewers

Makes 4 Servings

Hands On: 15 minutes
Unsupervised: 35 minutes

2 tablespoons hoisin sauce*

1 tablespoon ketchup

1 1/2 teaspoon tamari sauce

1/2 teaspoon sesame oil*

1 teaspoon Chinese chili sauce with garlic

1 1/2 teaspoon orange zest*

1/2 cup orange juice

1 1/2 pounds skinless, boneless chicken breast

In a bowl, add all ingredients except chicken. Mix well.

Cut chicken into 1-inch pieces. Add chicken to the marinade. Chill in refrigerator for 30 minutes.

Place 4 to 5 pieces of chicken onto each bamboo skewers. Broil over coals (about 5 minutes). Turn to cook evenly. Serve hot.

Approximate Nutrient Content per Serving

Calories	230
Fat	3 g
Saturated Fat	0.5 g
Cholesterol	100 mg
Sodium	600 mg
Carbohydrate	9 g
Protein	40 g

This is a great recipe for home, the beach, or tail-gate parties. Place the chicken in the marinade and put it in an iced cooler. It will be ready for the coals when you arrive.

Ikaika's Chow Fun

Makes 8 Servings

Hands On: 35 minutes
Unsupervised: 5 minutes

$^1/_2$ pound skinless, boneless chicken breast

I teaspoon reduced sodium soy sauce plus $^1/_2$ cup

$^1/_2$ teaspoon garlic powder

I teaspoon grated ginger*

2 cloves garlic, minced

I teaspoon sesame seed oil

6 cups frozen chop suey vegetables*

2 cups julienned cabbage

I cup sliced mushrooms

$^1/_2$ cup julienned char siu*

4 cups refrigerated chow fun noodles*

$^1/_2$ cup Yoshida's® gourmet sauce

$^1/_2$ cup reduced sodium soy sauce

2 teaspoons hot chili paste*

2 tablespoons katsu* sauce

Approximate Nutrient Content per Serving

Calories	250
Fat	2.5 g
Saturated Fat	0 g
Cholesterol	35 mg
Sodium	1410 mg
Carbohydrate	42 g
Protein	15 g

Cut chicken into strips.

In a wok, combine 1 teaspoon soy sauce, garlic powder, and ginger. Add chicken. Heat wok over medium high and stir-fry chicken for 3 to 5 minutes. Add garlic, sesame seed oil, and chop suey vegetables. Stir-fry for 2 minutes. Add all remaining vegetables, char siu, and noodles. Stir fry for 5 minutes.

Add gourmet sauce, chili paste, $^1/_2$ cup soy sauce and katsu sauce to noodles. Toss gently. Serve immediately.

This recipe was created for and named after our grandson Ikaika Salvador. Use only the fresh refrigerated chow fun noodles, dried noodles are processed with fat.

Chicken Caesar Salad ♥

Hands On: 25 minutes
Unsupervised: 25 minutes

2 tablespoons white wine

$1/_2$ teaspoon Dijon country mustard

$1/_8$ teaspoon milled black pepper*

8 ounces skinless, boneless chicken breast

4 cloves garlic, 1 smashed, 3 cloves minced

12 slices French bread, $1/_4$-inch thick

1 egg

2 tablespoons fresh lemon juice

1 anchovy filet, rinsed and chopped

$1/_4$ cup balsamic vinegar*

$1/_8$ teaspoon milled black pepper*

2 teaspoon olive oil

2 tablespoons grated nonfat parmesan cheese

12 cups torn romaine lettuce

Preheat oven to 375 degrees F.

In small bowl, combine wine, mustard and pepper. Marinade chicken in mixture for at least 15 minutes.

In the meanwhile, rub smashed garlic over French bread. Place on baking sheet and bake for 10 to 12 minutes turning bread over once. Remove from oven. Set aside.

Heat skillet to medium high and dry sauté chicken for 6 minutes each side. Remove from skillet, cool, and slice in $1/_4$-inch strips. Set aside.

In a small pot bring 2 cups water to boil. Gently place egg (with no cracks) in boiling water. Remove pot from stove, cover, and let stand for 10 minutes. Remove egg from water and cool for 10 minutes.

Combine minced garlic, lemon juice, anchovy, vinegar, and black pepper. Add oil slowly while whipping to emulsify. Add coddled egg and whip; add half of the cheese.

Cut lettuce into bite-size pieces and place lettuce in large bowl. Toss with dressing to coat lettuce evenly. Divide onto plates. Top with chicken and remaining cheese. Place toasted bread on sides of dish. Serve immediately.

Approximate Nutrient Content per Serving

Calories	290
Fat	6 g
Saturated Fat	1.5 g
Cholesterol	55 mg
Sodium	540 mg
Carbohydrate	43 g
Protein	16 g

Sweet and Sour
Chicken Stir-Fry

Makes 8 Servings

Hands On: 20 minutes
Unsupervised: 30 minutes

$^1/_2$ cup Sweet and Sour Sauce
  (page 191)

1 teaspoon dry sherry

1 tablespoon reduced sodium
  soy sauce

2 teaspoons lemon zest*

1 teaspoon minced garlic

1 teaspoon cornstarch

1 teaspoon grated ginger*

2 pounds skinless, boneless
  chicken breast, diced

1 cup sliced green bell pepper

1 cup julienned onion

1 cup julienned carrot

1 piece lemon grass*, julienne

4 ounces fresh asparagus,
  sliced diagonally

$^1/_4$ cup slivered green onions

1 cup julienned red bell
  pepper

4 kaffir lime leaves*

1 can (15 ounces) straw
  mushrooms, drained and
  rinsed

**Approximate Nutrient
Content per Serving**

Calories	300
Fat	2 g
Saturated Fat	0 g
Cholesterol	65 mg
Sodium	630 mg
Carbohydrate	44 g
Protein	29 g

Prepare Sweet and Sour Sauce.

Combine sherry, soy sauce, zest, garlic, cornstarch, and ginger. Add chicken and marinate for 30 minutes.

Heat wok. Stir-fry chicken with marinade, adding vegetables in order listed. Toss gently for 7 minutes.

Add sweet and sour sauce, heat thoroughly and serve over rice or noodles.

Kaffir leaves add a lime flavor. Like bay leaves, Kaffir leaves should be removed before serving to prevent family and guests from accidentally choking on stiff leaves.

Chicken Beggar's Pouch Over Taro with Pineapple, Papaya, Poha Relish ♥ Makes 4 Servings

Hands On: 15 minutes
Unsupervised: 60 minutes

1 cup Pineapple, Papaya*, Poha Relish (next page)

1 pound raw taro*

10 seconds vegetable oil spray

8 ounces skinless, boneless chicken breast, diced

1/2 cup chopped onions

2 teaspoons hot chili paste*

2 teaspoons minced garlic

1 tablespoon julienned ginger*

1 tablespoon reduced sodium soy sauce

1/2 cup julienned fresh shiitake mushrooms*

1 piece lemon grass*, thinly sliced

1/2 cup julienned carrots

4 tablespoons lime juice

3 phyllo dough sheets

1 tablespoon lime zest*

Approximate Nutrient Content per Serving

Calories	350
Fat	4 g
Saturated Fat	4 g
Cholesterol	35 mg
Sodium	380 mg
Carbohydrate	64 g
Protein	18 g

Prepare Pineapple, Papaya, Poha Relish.

Steam taro until fork can be easily inserted like a cooked potato (for 20 minutes). Trim skin and slice into 1/2-inch discs. Each piece is 3 to 4 ounces.

Lightly spray wok with vegetable oil spray (3 seconds). Stir-fry chicken with onions, chili paste, garlic, ginger, and soy sauce for 4 minutes over medium heat.

Add mushrooms, lemon grass, carrots, and lime juice and simmer for 5 minutes. (Save lime zest for garnish). Preheat oven to 375 degrees F.

Stack phyllo sheets together and spray between each layer (4 seconds total). Cut into 4 pieces about 6-inch square.

Place 1/2 cup of chicken mixture in center of each square and pull corners and edges up to form a pouch. Pinch phyllo an inch from the top, vegetable oil spray will help hold it together. Spray vegetable oil (3 seconds) very lightly over outside of pouches. Place on ungreased baking sheet and bake until phyllo is golden brown (about 10 minutes).

Place taro on plate, put beggars' pouches on taro. Drizzle 2 ounces relish on outer edge of taro and sprinkle with lime zest.

To keep phyllo dough from drying, keep covered with plastic when at room temperature.

Pineapple, Papaya, Poha Relish ♥

Makes 2¼ cups

Hands On: 15 minutes
Chill Time: 1 hour

1 cup minced pineapple*

½ cup minced papaya*

¼ cup poha berry*
  preserve

¼ cup minced red onion

1 teaspoon minced
  habañero chili pepper*

1 tablespoon chopped mint
  leaves

1 tablespoon orange juice

1 tablespoon rice vinegar*

1 tablespoon chopped
  cilantro*

Combine all ingredients and mix well.
Refrigerate for 1 hour before using so that
flavors have time to blend.

**Approximate Nutrient
Content per 2 Tablespoons**

Calories	30
Fat	0 g
Saturated Fat	0 g
Cholesterol	0 mg
Sodium	0 mg
Carbohydrate	8 g
Protein	0 g

Use ripe papayas and pineapples for this relish.

Mango-Sauced Chicken ❤

Makes 6 Servings

Hands On: 20 minutes
Unsupervised: 5 minutes

¾ cup Mango Vinaigrette
(next page)

1½ pounds skinless,
boneless chicken breast

1 pound fresh asparagus

1 red bell pepper

¾ cup fat-free, reduced
sodium chicken broth

2 teaspoons lemon zest*

1 tablespoon lemon juice

1 tablespoon reduced
sodium soy sauce

1½ tablespoons cornstarch

1 teaspoon sugar

½ teaspoon milled black
pepper*

3 seconds vegetable oil
spray

¾ cup diced mango*

Prepare Mango Vinaigrette.

Cut chicken into bite-size pieces. Cut asparagus in 1½ inch pieces and cut bell peppers into
1½-inch diamond shapes.

Combine broth, zest, lemon juice, soy sauce,
cornstarch, sugar, and black pepper. Set aside.

In a non-stick wok, add chicken and stir-fry
over high heat for 4 minutes until chicken turns
white. Add liquid broth mixture, lower heat to
medium and allow to simmer and thicken slightly.

Spray a smaller wok with vegetable oil spray.
Over high heat, add asparagus and bell pepper,
stir-fry for 4 minutes. Add mango vinaigrette and
diced mango. Heat for 1 minute.

Add vegetables and mango mixture to
chicken. Fold in evenly and simmer for 2 minutes.

Approximate Nutrient Content per Serving

Calories	190
Fat	2 g
Saturated Fat	0 g
Cholesterol	65 mg
Sodium	310 mg
Carbohydrate	13 g
Protein	29 g

Flavors blend wonderfully with brown rice.

Mango Vinaigrette

Makes 2³/₄ cups

Hands On: 15 minutes

1 ¹/₂ cups chopped ripe
    mangoes*

1 clove garlic

1 tablespoon chopped
    onion

¹/₈ teaspoon hot chili paste*

1 teaspoon soy sauce

1 ¹/₂ teaspoon lime juice

²/₃ cup rice vinegar*

¹/₂ cup water

1 teaspoon salt

¹/₂ teaspoon milled black
    pepper*

Puree all ingredients in a food processor until mixture is smooth.

Refrigerate until needed.

**Approximate Nutrient
Content per 2 Tablespoons**

Calories	10
Fat	0 g
Saturated Fat	0 g
Cholesterol	0 mg
Sodium	110 mg
Carbohydrate	2 g
Protein	0 g

In Hawai'i, the most common varieties of mango are Hayden, common, Pirie and Chinese. For this recipe, use the Hayden.

Honey-Shoyu Chicken ❤

Makes 6 Servings

Hands On: 20 minutes
Unsupervised: 2 hours

6 skinless chicken breasts
with bone (6 ounces
each)

Marinade Ingredients:

$^1/_2$ cup dry white wine

2 tablespoons honey

3 cloves garlic, minced

1 tablespoon grated
ginger*

2 tablespoons lemon juice

$^1/_4$ cup orange juice

$^1/_4$ cup chopped green
onions

2 tablespoons reduced
sodium soy sauce,

3 seconds vegetable oil
spray

Remove all visible fat from chicken.

Combine wine, honey, garlic, ginger, juices, green onions, and soy sauce. Place chicken in marinade in refrigerator for at least 2 hours. Turn occasionally.

Remove chicken from marinade. Lightly spray skillet with vegetable oil spray and cook chicken over medium heat for 4 to 5 minutes each side. Serve hot. Also excellent grilled over hot coals.

**Approximate Nutrient
Content per Serving**

Calories	170
Fat	2 g
Saturated Fat	0 g
Cholesterol	65 mg
Sodium	280 mg
Carbohydrate	9 g
Protein	26 g

Non-alcoholic version is possible by substituting rice vinegar for white wine.

Chicken Curry
Three Mushrooms ♥

Makes 8 Servings

Hands On: 15 minutes
Unsupervised: 25 minutes

8 seconds vegetable oil
spray

¹/₂ cup diced carrots

¹/₂ cup diced celery

¹/₂ cup diced onions

2 tablespoons curry
powder

1 cup sliced shiitake
mushrooms*

1 cup straw mushrooms

1 cup button mushrooms

2 pounds skinless, boneless
chicken breast, diced

3 cups fat-free, reduced
sodium chicken broth

2 cups skim milk

2 cups water

¹/₂ cup cornstarch

2 cups diced apples

Lightly spray a large pot with vegetable oil and heat. Sauté carrots, celery, onions, and curry powder and cook for 5 minutes. Add mushrooms and chicken, cook for another 5 minutes. Add 2 cups broth, milk, and water. Simmer for 20 minutes.

Stir cornstarch into 1 cup cold broth and blend until smooth. Add cornstarch mixture to chicken mixture, stir constantly until it thickens.

Add apples and simmer for 5 minutes. Remove from heat and serve hot.

**Approximate Nutrient
Content per Serving**

Calories	240
Fat	3 g
Saturated Fat	0.5 g
Cholesterol	65 mg
Sodium	480 mg
Carbohydrate	22 g
Protein	31 g

Not all curries are the same. Curry powders are made of 7 to 14 different spices and herbs. Many regions of the world blend their own combination of these spices and herbs producing unique curry flavors.

Chicken Papaya, Pumpkin and Summer Squash

Makes 6 Servings

Hands On: 15 minutes
Unsupervised: 30 minutes

¹/₂ cup sliced dried shiitake mushroom*

3 cups water

12 ounces skinless chicken breast with bone, cut into 8 pieces

3 cups stew cut carrots

5 cups fat-free, reduced sodium chicken broth

2 stalks celery, cut into large pieces

1 cup diced onion

2 cups diced pumpkin squash

2 cups diced summer squash

2 cups diced green papaya*

2 thumb-size ginger* root, sliced length-wise

2 cloves garlic, minced

1 teaspoon salt

¹/₄ cup chopped parsley

Soak shiitake mushrooms in 2 cups water. Drain when reconstituted.

In a large pot, add 1 cup of water, chicken, and carrots. Simmer for 10 minutes.

Add broth, mushrooms, celery, onion, pumpkin, summer squash, papaya, ginger root, garlic, and salt. Simmer covered for 20 minutes or until squash is tender.

Serve hot and garnish with chopped parsley.

Approximate Nutrient Content per Serving

Calories	130
Fat	1 g
Saturated Fat	0 g
Cholesterol	20 mg
Sodium	920 mg
Carbohydrate	18 g
Protein	14 g

This is similar to the soup-type entree called chicken papaya known well to those from the Philippines.

Apple Cider Chicken and Golden Raisins ♥

Makes 5 Servings

Hands On: 20 minutes
Unsupervised: 10 minutes

3 tablespoons flour

$^1/_2$ teaspoon salt

$^1/_4$ teaspoon milled black pepper*

$^1/_4$ teaspoon cinnamon

$1^1/_2$ pounds skinless, boneless chicken breast, stew cut

5 seconds vegetable oil spray

$1^1/_2$ cup apple cider

1 tablespoon cornstarch

1 tablespoon water

$2^1/_2$ cups diced Granny Smith apples with peel

$^1/_2$ cup golden raisins

$^1/_4$ cup skim milk

2 tablespoons lime juice

1 teaspoon lime zest*

$^1/_4$ cup chopped parsley

In a bowl, combine flour, salt, pepper, and cinnamon. Dredge chicken pieces in flour mixture and shake off excess flour.

Spray skillet lightly with vegetable oil spray. Heat to medium high, then add chicken. Cook for 3 to 5 minutes, turn to cook evenly to golden brown. Remove chicken from skillet.

To skillet, add cider and heat to simmer. Stir in cornstarch and water until a creamy consistency is reached. Add apples and raisins, cover and simmer on low heat for 5 minutes. Add chicken and simmer for 3 more minutes.

Slowly add milk to chicken mixture, then lime juice and zest. Garnish with chopped parsley.

Approximate Nutrient Content per Serving

Calories	270
Fat	3 g
Saturated Fat	0.5 g
Cholesterol	80 mg
Sodium	330 mg
Carbohydrate	27 g
Protein	33 g

The blend of apples, cinnamon, apple cider, and raisins combined with chicken goes exceptionally well with brown rice.

Chicken Stew and Dumplings

Makes 6 Servings

Hands On: 40 minutes
Unsupervised: 30 minutes

Dumpling Recipe (next page)

1 teaspoon canola oil

$1/_2$ cup diced onions

$1/_2$ cup diced carrots

$1/_2$ cup diced celery

1 parsnip, peeled, diced

$1/_2$ cup cut corn kernels

$1/_2$ cup leeks, diced

2 bay leaves

2 teaspoons oregano

2 teaspoons basil

$1/_4$ cup diced plum tomato

$1/_2$ cup diced red bell pepper

20 ounces beef broth

10 ounces fat-free, reduced sodium chicken broth

1 tablespoon hot chili paste*

12 ounces skinless, boneless chicken breast, cut in strips

6 ounces okra, sliced

Prepare Dumpling Recipe.

In a large stockpot add oil, onions, carrots, celery, parsnip, corn, leeks, and sauté until they begin to sweat and become tender (about 6 minutes). Add bay leaves, oregano, basil and plum tomato and sauté 2 more minutes.

Add bell peppers and both broths and bring to a boil. Add chili paste and chicken. When liquid begins to boil again, lower heat to a low simmer. Add okra, cover pot and simmer for 10 minutes.

Dumpling dough can be added to stew at this time. Bring stew to a boil and drop dumplings into liquid, cover pot, and lower heat to a fast simmer for 20 minutes. (Note: If broth evaporates and there is not enough liquid to cover dumplings, remove some of the chicken and vegetables before adding the dumplings to the pot. Keep chicken warm until dumplings are cooked, then add the chicken and vegetables back to the pot.)

Approximate Nutrient Content per Serving

Calories	260
Fat	4 g
Saturated Fat	1 g
Cholesterol	70 mg
Sodium	800 mg
Carbohydrate	36 g
Protein	23 g

Dumplings ♥

Hands On: 10 minutes
Unsupervised: 20 minutes

$^1/_4$ cup apple sauce

$^1/_4$ cup buttermilk

$^1/_4$ cup fat-free egg substitute

1 teaspoon vegetable oil

1 $^1/_2$ cup wheat flour

1 teaspoon salt

$^1/_4$ teaspoon baking soda

$^1/_2$ teaspoon sugar

1 tablespoon chopped parsley

Combine apple sauce, buttermilk, egg, and oil and mix well.

In separate bowl combine flour, salt, baking soda, sugar, and parsley and mix well. Making a well in the flour mixture, pour liquid mixture into well. Gently fold flour mixture from edge of bowl under to the center of the liquid in the well bringing up the flour through the center of the well. Incorporate the liquid ingredients as the mixture is folded together. Do not over-mix or press down, this will make dumplings tough and heavy. Cover and chill.

When all ingredients have been added to the stew, turn dumpling dough onto floured board and roll out to $^3/_4$-inch thickness. Cut into 1$^1/_2$ inch pieces. Bring stew to a boil and drop dumplings into liquid, cover pot and lower heat to a fast simmer for 20 minutes.

Approximate Nutrient Content per Serving

Calories	130
Fat	2 g
Saturated Fat	0 g
Cholesterol	35 mg
Sodium	430 mg
Carbohydrate	24 g
Protein	6 g

Even though chicken and dumplings is no longer a standard home-cooked meal, children still love them. And because the recipe is easy, it can be added to any stew.

Capistrano Breast of Chicken ❤

Makes 4 Servings

Hands On: 15 minutes
Unsupervised: 20 minutes

1/2 cup wheat flour

1 tablespoon taco seasoning

1 teaspoon black pepper

4 skinless, boneless chicken breasts (4-ounces each)

3 seconds vegetable oil spray

1/4 cup finely diced onion

1/4 cup frozen margarita mix concentrate, thawed

1/4 cup vermouth

1/2 cup orange juice

1/2 cup juice of canned whole plum tomatoes

1/2 cup corn kernels

1/4 cup sliced black olives

1/2 cup canned whole plum tomatoes

4 tablespoons grated Monterey Jack cheese

1 tablespoon orange zest*

1 tablespoon diced cilantro*

Combine flour, taco seasoning, and pepper; mix well. Dust chicken with flour mixture.

Spray skillet lightly with vegetable oil. Heat skillet to medium high for 30 seconds. Place floured chicken in skillet. Cook for 3 minutes to brown, then turn chicken over and brown second side for 3 minutes.

Add onions, cook until transparent and slightly brown. Add margarita mix, let liquid loosen floured chicken particles from skillet. Add vermouth and orange juice, simmer 5 minutes, then add juice of plum tomatoes. Simmer for 5 more minutes. Add corn, olives and plum tomatoes, simmer for 10 minutes. Sprinkle 1 tablespoon cheese on each chicken breast. Add a sprinkle of orange zest and cilantro* and serve.

Approximate Nutrient Content per Serving

Calories	320
Fat	6 g
Saturated Fat	2 g
Cholesterol	70 mg
Sodium	390 mg
Carbohydrate	30 g
Protein	32 g

This recipe started out from ingredients in our refrigerator. The original recipe used orange oil, but with a little experimenting, we found that orange juice concentrate worked just as well. On the day this recipe was created, swallows returned to Capistrano and hence the intriguing name.

Chicken Cannelloni

Makes 4 Servings

Hands On: 15 minutes
Unsupervised: 30 minutes

1³/₄ cups Marinara Sauce I
(page 192)

8 cannelloni tubes*

¹/₂ cup skim evaporated milk

1 cup fresh white bread
crumbs

³/₄ pound skinless, boneless
chicken breast

2 tablespoons diced shallots

2 cloves garlic, minced

2 egg whites

¹/₂ teaspoon salt

¹/₄ teaspoon white pepper

¹/₄ teaspoon cayenne

¹/₄ teaspoon fresh thyme

¹/₄ teaspoon fresh basil

¹/₂ cup diced celery

¹/₂ cup sliced mushrooms

5 seconds vegetable oil spray

2 tablespoons chopped
parsley

Prepare Marinara Sauce I.

Preheat oven to 375 degrees F.

Cook cannelloni tubes according to package to al dente*. Do not over cook. Rinse, drain, and set aside.

Heat milk to simmer. Add bread crumbs and simmer for 2 additional minutes. Set aside to cool.

In food processor, puree chicken, shallots, garlic, and egg whites. Add milk-bread mixture, peppers, chopped thyme, and basil. Mix well.

Remove from processor. Fold in diced celery and mushrooms.

Prepare baking dish with vegetable oil spray. Spoon chicken mixture into cannelloni tubes. Place stuffed tubes in baking dish and ladle marinara sauce over the top of the pasta. Cover with baking paper and bake for 30 minutes. Remove from oven and place on dishes and garnish with chopped parsley. Serve hot.

Approximate Nutrient Content per Serving

Calories	440
Fat	6 g
Saturated Fat	1 g
Cholesterol	50 mg
Sodium	710 mg
Carbohydrate	61 g
Protein	31 g

Turkey Hungarian Goulash with Seasoned Parsley Egg Noodles

Makes 8 Servings

Hands On: 15 minutes
Unsupervised: 15 minutes

Seasoned Parsley Egg
   Noodles (next page)

1³/₄ cup fat-free, reduced
   sodium chicken broth

4 cloves garlic, minced

1 cup diced onion

1 cup diced leek, white only

4 cups diced skinless,
   boneless turkey breast

2 tablespoons Dijon mustard

2 tablespoons Hungarian
   paprika

¹/₂ teaspoon milled black
   pepper*

1¹/₂ teaspoons whole thyme
   leaves

³/₄ pound button mushrooms

1 can (6 ounces) tomato
   paste

1 diced green bell pepper

³/₄ cup nonfat sour cream

³/₄ cup plain low-fat yogurt

¹/₃ cup chopped parsley

Prepare Seasoned Parsley Egg Noodles.

Heat large sauce pot. Add ³/₄ cup broth and bring to a boil. Add garlic, onions, and leek and cook for 5 minutes.

Add turkey, and stir while cooking on medium heat for 5 minutes. Add mustard, paprika, black pepper, and thyme and cook for 7 minutes. Stir occasionally.

Add mushrooms, tomato paste, bell pepper, and remaining broth. Cook on low heat for 8 minutes and stir constantly to prevent the bottom from burning.

Mix sour cream and yogurt. Add half of this mixture to goulash. Blend well.

Serve goulash over hot noodles. Top with a dollop of the remaining sour cream-yogurt mixture and chopped parsley.

**Approximate Nutrient
Content per Serving**

Calories	370
Fat	4 g
Saturated Fat	1 g
Cholesterol	95 mg
Sodium	490 mg
Carbohydrate	53 g
Protein	32 g

There are two different types of Hungarian paprika - mild and really hot. Use the type that suits you.

Seasoned Parsley Egg Noodles ❤

Hands On: 5 minutes
Unsupervised: 10 minutes

³/₄ gallon water

1 pound egg noodles
(without egg yolks)

1 tablespoon Fleischman's®
nonfat, no cholesterol
butter flavor (in squeeze
bottle)

2 tablespoons chopped
parsley

1 tablespoon milled black
pepper*

Bring water to boil. Add noodles. Stir and cook for 10 minutes.

Drain well in colander, then add back into same pot that has been drained completely.

Add to noodles, butter flavor, parsley and black pepper. Toss to coat evenly over noodles. Serve on plates while hot.

Approximate Nutrient Content per Serving

Calories	190
Fat	2 g
Saturated Fat	0 g
Cholesterol	45 mg
Sodium	25 mg
Carbohydrate	35 g
Protein	7 g

This goes well with lots of dishes.

Turkey Cutlet with Cranberry Relish ❤

Makes 4 Servings

Hands On: 25 minutes
Unsupervised: 10 minutes

³/₄ cup Cranberry Relish (next page)

1 pound skinless, boneless turkey breast

3 tablespoons flour

1 teaspoon salt

¹/₂ teaspoon black pepper

1 teaspoon oregano

¹/₂ teaspoon sage

4 seconds vegetable oil spray

¹/₄ cup orange juice

Prepare Cranberry Relish.

Cut turkey breast into 8 pieces. Place each piece between 2 sheets of heavy plastic wrap. Using a mallet, flatten to ¹/₈-inch thickness.

Combine and blend evenly, flour, salt, pepper, oregano, and sage. Dredge turkey cutlet in flour mixture.

Lightly spray skillet with vegetable oil spray. Heat skillet on medium heat and cook turkey for 2 to 3 minutes each side. While cutlets are still in skillet, add orange juice and simmer for 8 to 10 minutes.

Serve 2 cutlets per person with 3 tablespoons of cranberry relish.

Approximate Nutrient Content per Serving

Calories	220
Fat	2 g
Saturated Fat	0 g
Cholesterol	70 mg
Sodium	590 mg
Carbohydrate	22 g
Protein	29 g

Both the cranberry relish and thinly sliced turkey freeze well. So this recipe is an ideal quick, yet special meal.

Cranberry Relish ♥

Hands On: 15 minutes
Unsupervised: 10 minutes

1 pound fresh cranberries
1/2 cup honey
1 1/3 cup fresh orange juice
4 tablespoons orange zest*

Combine all ingredients in sauce pot. Heat to a boil; then simmer for 10 minutes.
Remove from heat and cool.
Refrigerate until ready to serve.

**Approximate Nutrient
Content per 2 Tablespoons**

Calories	40
Fat	0 g
Saturated Fat	0 g
Cholesterol	0 mg
Sodium	0 mg
Carbohydrate	10 g
Protein	0 g

Chicken Marsala ♥

1 pound skinless, boneless chicken breast

$^1\!/_4$ cup flour

$^1\!/_2$ teaspoon salt

$^1\!/_4$ teaspoon milled black pepper*

1 teaspoon olive oil

$^1\!/_3$ cup fat-free, reduced sodium chicken broth

$2^1\!/_2$ cup sliced mushrooms

1/2 cup marsala

1 tablespoon chopped parsley

Cut chicken into 8 pieces. Place chicken between 2 sheets of heavy plastic wrap and flatten with a mallet to $^1\!/_8$-inch thickness.

Mix flour, salt and pepper.

Dredge chicken in 3 tablespoons of flour mixture.

In medium size skillet, heat oil to medium temperature. Add chicken and cook for 4 minutes each side. Remove from skillet, pat excess oil with paper towels.

In the same skillet, sauté mushrooms and broth, simmer for 2 minutes. Blend in remaining flour and cook 5 minutes.

Add marsala to mushroom mixture and simmer 5 minutes. Return chicken to skillet, cover and simmer 5 more minutes.

Garnish with just a sprinkle of parsley.

Approximate Nutrient Content per Serving

Calories	220
Fat	3 g
Saturated Fat	0.5 g
Cholesterol	65 mg
Sodium	390 mg
Carbohydrate	12 g
Protein	28 g

Elegant, yet simple to prepare. Perfect for a candle light dinner.

Turkey Lasagna

Makes 8 Servings

Hands On: 20 minutes
Unsupervised: 40 minutes

9 lasagna noodles

6 seconds vegetable oil spray

I pound ground turkey

$^1/_2$ cup chopped red bell pepper

$^1/_2$ cup chopped onion

3 cloves garlic, chopped

I cup tomato sauce

I can (6 ounces) tomato paste

$^1/_2$ cup water

$^1/_4$ teaspoon salt

$^1/_4$ teaspoon dried whole thyme

$^1/_4$ teaspoon ground oregano

I $^1/_2$ cups low-fat cottage cheese

$^1/_2$ cup part-skim shredded
mozzarella

20 ounces frozen chopped
spinach, thawed

3 tablespoons dried bread
crumbs

2 tablespoons chopped parsley

$^1/_2$ teaspoon paprika

Approximate Nutrient Content per Serving

Calories	300
Fat	8 g
Saturated Fat	3 g
Cholesterol	50 mg
Sodium	750 mg
Carbohydrate	33 g
Protein	25 g

Prepare lasagna noodles as per package directions. Preheat oven to 350 degrees F.

Lightly spray skillet with vegetable oil spray. Heat to medium- high. Add turkey, peppers, onion, and garlic. Sauté until brown. Drain liquid from skillet.

Add tomato sauce, paste, water, salt, thyme, and oregano to skillet and heat mixture to a simmer. Cover and simmer for 20 minutes.

In a small bowl, mix cottage cheese and mozzarella.

Squeeze liquid out of spinach and blend into cheese mixture.

Lightly spray 11 x 7 x 2-inch baking dish with vegetable oil spray. Lay 3 lasagna noodles on bottom. Spoon half of turkey mixture evenly over noodles and cover with 3 noodles. Evenly spread half of the spinach mixture and cover with remaining 3 noodles. Spread top with remaining turkey and cheese-spinach mixtures and sprinkle top with dried bread crumbs, parsley, and paprika.

Cover pan with aluminum foil or baking paper and bake for 20 minutes. Uncover and bake for 10 more minutes. Cool slightly before cutting and serving.

Vermicelli with Turkey, Basil, and Plum Tomato ❤

Makes 4 Servings

Hands On: 20 minutes
Unsupervised: 15 minutes

8 ounces dry vermicelli

3 seconds vegetable oil spray

3 cloves garlic, chopped

$1/2$ cup diced onions

$1/2$ cup diced green bell peppers

$1/2$ cup diced zucchini

2 cups peeled, seeded, and quarter plum tomatoes

$1/4$ cup dry white wine

2 teaspoons capers*

1 cup fat-free, reduced sodium chicken broth

2 cups shredded, cooked white turkey

$1/2$ cup chopped fresh basil leaves

Cook vermicelli according to package directions. Drain and set aside.

Lightly spray sauté pan with vegetable oil spray. Sauté garlic and onions until soft. Add bell peppers and zucchini; sauté for 3 minutes. Add tomatoes, wine, and capers; simmer for 5 minutes. Add broth, pasta, turkey, and basil. Cook until evenly heated (about 5 minutes).

Serve.

Approximate Nutrient Content per Serving

Calories	370
Fat	2 g
Saturated Fat	0 g
Cholesterol	60 mg
Sodium	240 mg
Carbohydrate	53 g
Protein	33 g

Vermicelli is longer and thinner than spaghetti. Although not changing the flavors of the dish, using vermicelli changes the mouth-feel of the dish.

Pork, Veal, Beef

To include these meats in recipes and still meet the "low-fat" definition, this section is comprised of recipes containing higher priced cuts of meats, such as pork loin instead of pork butt and round tip beef instead of chuck roast. Keeping in mind that meat in these recipes will cost a little more, we combined these higher priced ingredients with other affordable ingredients. Again, there are "local" type recipes as well as from the Americas, Asia, Europe, and Northern Africa.

Sometimes leaner meats are also tougher cuts. With this in mind, potential tougher cuts of meat require slightly different cooking techniques to tenderize. We've used techniques such as cutting meats against the grain, stewing, braising, and marinating meats overnight. We are confident you will enjoy the culinary results of these dishes.

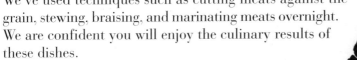

Roast Pork Loin with Dried Fruit Stuffing ❤

Makes 18 Servings

Hands On: 25 minutes
Unsupervised: 40 minutes

3 cups Shiitake Sauce Recipe (next page)

I cup orange juice

I cup dried whole cranberries

2 cups diced mixed dried fruits

4¹/₂ cups fat-free, reduced sodium chicken broth

¹/₂ cup diced onion

¹/₂ cup diced celery

I teaspoon sage

4 cups diced wheat bread

4 egg whites

3¹/₂ pounds lean pork loin, butterflied by butcher

2 teaspoons garlic salt

2 teaspoons milled black pepper*

Prepare double the Shiitake Sauce Recipe.

Preheat oven to 425 degrees F.

Heat orange juice, cranberries, and mixed fruits to boil 5 minutes. Remove from heat and set aside.

In a large sauce pot, heat 2¹/₂ cups broth, add onion, celery, and sage. Cook for 5 minutes. Remove from heat. Add bread and egg whites and mix together. Add fruit mixture to bread mixture and mix well.

Lay pork loin flat on cutting board. Season with garlic salt and pepper. Spread bread stuffing over pork. Firmly roll-up pork and wrap with aluminum foil and seal well. Place pork loin in baking dish with remaining 2 cups broth. Bake for 25 to 35 minutes.

Slice pork into ¹/₂-inch slices and serve with 3 tablespoons shiitake mushroom sauce.

Approximate Nutrient Content per Serving

Calories	250
Fat	6 g
Saturated Fat	1.5 g
Cholesterol	55 mg
Sodium	440 mg
Carbohydrate	27 g
Protein	23 g

Ask your butcher for special cuts. This is a great way to decrease your time in the kitchen.

Shiitake Sauce

Makes 3 cups

Hands On: 10 minutes
Unsupervised: 5 minutes

$^1/_2$ cup white wine

2 cloves garlic, minced

2 cups sliced fresh shiitake
mushrooms*

1 cup fat-free, reduced
sodium chicken broth

2 tablespoons cornstarch

2 tablespoons water

$^1/_2$ cup sliced green onions

1 teaspoon milled black
pepper*

Pour wine into sauce pan and heat. Add garlic and simmer for 3 minutes.

Add mushrooms and broth. Simmer for 5 minutes.

Mix cornstarch and water to make a paste.

Stir paste into other ingredients to thicken.

Add green onions and pepper. Serve.

**Approximate Nutrient
Content per $^1/_4$ cup**

Calories	30
Fat	0 g
Saturated Fat	0 g
Cholesterol	0 mg
Sodium	50 mg
Carbohydrate	5 g
Protein	1 g

Fresh shiitake mushrooms can be savored in this simple sauce.

Maple Rum
Pork Medallions ♥

Makes 8 Servings

Hands On: 20 minutes
Unsupervised: 10 minutes

1/3 cup maple syrup

1/3 cup apple juice

1/3 cup vegetable broth

2 tablespoons whole grain mustard

2 tablespoons ketchup

3 seconds vegetable oil spray

1 1/2 pound trimmed pork loin, cut into 12 slices

2 tablespoons rum

6 cups broccoli florets

Combine in small bowl maple syrup, apple juice, vegetable broth, mustard, and ketchup. Mix well. Set aside.

Lightly spray sauté pan with vegetable oil spray. Heat pan and cook pork slices for 4 minutes on each side. Remove pork.

Bring pan away from heat. Add rum. Allow the rum to lift off the residue of pork in pan from cooking. Add the maple syrup mixture to pan then return pan to heat and cook for 5 minutes.

Add pork back to pan and simmer for 10 minutes.

Steam broccoli florets.

Serve hot.

**Approximate Nutrient
Content per Serving**

Calories	200
Fat	5 g
Saturated Fat	1.5 g
Cholesterol	55 mg
Sodium	310 mg
Carbohydrate	16 g
Protein	21 g

Caution: Medium heat from burner will ignite rum. Therefore, the pan should be moved away from the heat and slightly cooled before pouring measured rum amount into pan. Carefully return pan back to burner without splashing liquid.

Ground Pork and Eggplant-Hunan Style ♥

Makes 4 Servings

Hands On: 15 minutes
Unsupervised: 5 minutes

4 ounces ground lean pork

3 seconds vegetable oil spray

1 clove garlic, chopped

6 cups sliced Japanese eggplant*

1 teaspoon hot chili paste*

2 teaspoons grated ginger*

2 cloves garlic, chopped

1/2 cup fat-free, reduced sodium chicken broth

2 tablespoons reduced sodium soy sauce

1 tablespoon mirin* or rice vinegar*

1 teaspoon sugar

1 teaspoon cornstarch

1 teaspoon water

In a non-stick pan, heat and sauté pork and garlic for 5 minutes. Remove pork and drain oil. Set aside.

Away from heat, lightly spray pan with vegetable oil spray. Heat and sauté eggplant. Add chili paste, ginger, and garlic and stir. Stir-fry until eggplant is soft (3 to 4 minutes). Add broth, soy sauce, mirin, and sugar. Simmer for 3 minutes.

Mix cornstarch and water. Add to eggplant and stir. Add pork and heat thoroughly stirring until sauce thickens slightly.

Serve hot.

Approximate Nutrient Content per Serving

Calories	110
Fat	3 g
Saturated Fat	1 g
Cholesterol	10 mg
Sodium	480 mg
Carbohydrate	14 g
Protein	5 g

Food from the Hunan region of China is generally hotter than food from the Szechuan region. This recipe is written for local taste. Add 4 to 5 teaspoons of hot chili paste for Hunan hotness.

Yu-Shiang Pork

Makes 4 Servings

Hands On: 20 minutes
Unsupervised: 10 minutes

1 pound fat-trimmed pork loin

2 quarts water

2 slices ginger*, bruised

2 seconds vegetable oil spray

4 cloves garlic, minced

1/4 cup reduced sodium soy sauce

2 tablespoons mirin* or sherry

1 tablespoon sugar

1 cup fat-free, reduced sodium chicken broth

2 cups thinly sliced daikon*

2 cups thinly sliced carrots

1/2 cup thinly sliced bamboo shoots

1 tablespoon cornstarch

1 tablespoon water

1/2 cup 1-inch sliced green onions

Approximate Nutrient Content per Serving

Calories	260
Fat	7 g
Saturated Fat	2 g
Cholesterol	70 mg
Sodium	870 mg
Carbohydrate	20 g
Protein	29 g

Slice pork into 1-inch strips.

Bring water to a boil. Add ginger, simmer for 5 minutes. Add pork, simmer for 3 minutes. Drain and rinse pork.

Spray wok with vegetable oil spray. Add pork and garlic. Stir-fry for 3 minutes. Add soy sauce, mirin, sugar, and broth, simmer for 3 minutes.

Add daikon, carrots, and bamboo shoots, stir-fry for 5 minutes.

Combine cornstarch and water, add to wok and bring to a boil.

To serve, place on 4 individual dishes and garnish with green onions. Serve hot.

The original recipe, from the Shanghai region of China, uses pork butt and fresh bamboo shoots. Adding the carrots and daikon not only gives this dish texture and color, but also more acceptance from Hawai'i's local taste. Sherry can be substituted for mirin.

Veal Piccata ♥

Hands On: 25 minutes
Unsupervised: 5 minutes

4 1/2 cups cooked white rice
1 pound boneless veal loin
1 teaspoon salt
1/2 teaspoon ground pepper
2/3 cup all-purpose flour
4 seconds vegetable oil
    spray
1/2 cup dry white wine
1/2 cup beef broth
1 1/2 tablespoon lemon juice
1 teaspoon lemon zest*
1 teaspoon cornstarch
1 teaspoon water
1 tablespoon butter, soft
1 tablespoon chopped
    parsley
6 thin lemon slices

Slice veal into 12 thin pieces. Between 2 thick sheets of plastic, gently pound until veal becomes thin but not broken. Season with salt and pepper. Dust in flour.

Spray skillet with vegetable oil spray. Heat, add veal and cook quickly for about 2 minutes on each side. Remove veal.

To skillet, add wine and bring to boil, lifting any meat and flour particles from pan. When wine reduces by half, add lemon juice and zest. Continue to boil until liquid is reduced by half again.

Mix cornstarch with water. Add to reduced liquid and allow to thicken.

Remove skillet from heat. Swirl in butter to sauce and add parsley.

Place 2 pieces of veal on a plate with ³/₄ cup steamed rice. Ladle 3 tablespoons sauce over veal and garnish with lemon slice.

Approximate Nutrient Content per Serving

Calories	380
Fat	6 g
Saturated Fat	2 g
Cholesterol	65 mg
Sodium	510 mg
Carbohydrate	54 g
Protein	21 g

Veal piccata is a classic recipe. Although veal prices are usually higher than other meats, only small amounts of veal are served.

Veal Roast with Pear-Pepper Relish

Makes 8 Servings

Hands On: 15 minutes
Unsupervised: 90 hours

2 cups Pear-Pepper Relish (next page)

3 pounds boneless rolled veal rump roast

4 cloves garlic, chopped

1 tablespoon salt

1 tablespoon milled black pepper*

2 tablespoons fresh rosemary

4 seconds vegetable oil spray

1 cup dry white wine

$^1/_2$ cup beef broth

Prepare Pear-Pepper Relish recipe at least 8 hours prior to meal. Refrigerate.

Preheat oven to 325 degrees F.

Unroll roast, trim all fat. Rub garlic on inside of roast, season with salt, pepper, and rosemary. Roll roast and tie with butcher's twine to secure ends and center. Season outside with salt and pepper.

Lightly spray ovenproof dutch oven or roasting pan with vegetable oil spray. Place over medium high heat. When pan is hot, add rolled roast and brown on all sides. Add wine and broth. Cover pan and bake for 1$^1/_2$ hours. Baste every 20 minutes.

To serve, remove strings. Slice thin and serve with $^1/_4$ cup of pear-pepper relish.

Approximate Nutrient Content per Serving

Calories	260
Fat	6 g
Saturated Fat	1.5 g
Cholesterol	145 mg
Sodium	980 mg
Carbohydrate	12 g
Protein	35 g

This is a nice meal for Sunday dinner. Prepare the relish Saturday night, then season the roast and cook 1$^1/_2$ hours before dinner time. This roast is tender and moist and the relish is great.

Pear-Pepper Relish

Makes 3 cups

Hands On: 15 minutes
Unsupervised: 8 hours

2 cups finely diced fresh
    pears

$^1/_2$ cup canned whole
    cranberry sauce

$^1/_2$ cup finely diced green
    bell peppers

$^1/_4$ cup finely diced red
    onions

1 tablespoon balsamic
    vinegar*

1 tablespoon chopped
    chives

2 tablespoons lime juice

1 teaspoon chopped fresh
    thyme

Combine all ingredients and mix well. Cover and refrigerate for 8 hours or overnight.

**Approximate Nutrient
Content per 2 Tablespoons**

Calories	20
Fat	0 g
Saturated Fat	0 g
Cholesterol	0 mg
Sodium	0 mg
Carbohydrate	5 g
Protein	0 g

*Any variety of pear can be used. This relish
served cold gives meats a wonderful freshness.*

Veal Scaloppine with Marsala ❤

Makes 5 Servings

Hands On: 15 minutes
Unsupervised: 10 minutes

1 pound boneless veal loin

¼ cup flour

1 teaspoon salt

1 teaspoon milled black pepper*

4 seconds vegetable oil spray

½ cup beef broth

3 cups sliced mushrooms

½ cup marsala

1 tablespoon chopped parsley

Cut veal into 10 thin slices. Place between 2 sheets of heavy plastic and flatten to ⅛-inch thickness. Combine flour, salt and pepper and dredge veal evenly.

Lightly spray skillet with vegetable oil spray and heat to medium. Sauté veal for 3 minutes on each side and remove from skillet.

In same skillet, add broth, loosen flour and meat from pan and add mushrooms and marsala. Simmer until mushrooms are tender. Gradually stir in remaining flour until sauce thickens. Simmer for 7 minutes.

Return veal to sauce. Simmer for 2 minutes to warm veal thoroughly.

Garnish with chopped parsley and serve hot.

Approximate Nutrient Content per Serving

Calories	180
Fat	4 g
Saturated Fat	1 g
Cholesterol	75 mg
Sodium	590 mg
Carbohydrate	10 g
Protein	20 g

Constant stirring while adding flour will produce a smooth sauce.

Hilo Beef Stew

Hands On: 20 minutes
Unsupervised: 30 minutes

1 pound lean top round, stew cut

1 teaspoon black pepper

$\frac{1}{2}$ cup all-purpose flour

3 seconds vegetable oil spray

4 cloves garlic, chopped

$\frac{1}{2}$ cup diced onion

3 cups beef broth

1 cup water

2 teaspoons coarse Hawaiian salt

1 cup stew cut carrots

1 cup stew cut potatoes

1 cup stew cut celery

$\frac{1}{2}$ cup frozen peas

1 tablespoon Chili Pepper Water (page 196)

Season beef with pepper. Dredge in flour.

Spray large pot with vegetable oil spray. Sauté garlic and onions until soft. Add beef and brown on all sides. Add a little broth if beef sticks to pot. When beef is completely browned, add rest of broth, water and Hawaiian salt. Cover. Simmer for 15 minutes.

Add carrots, cover and simmer for 10 minutes. Add potatoes and celery and simmer for 10 minutes more.

To serve, ladle stew into soup bowls, garnish with peas and offer chili pepper water on the side to sprinkle into stew.

Approximate Nutrient Content per Serving

Calories	230
Fat	3.5 g
Saturated Fat	1 g
Cholesterol	50 mg
Sodium	1390 mg
Carbohydrate	23 g
Protein	26 g

On the Big Island, this type of stew is prepared in restaurants. No tomato paste or tomato sauce, but always the chili pepper water!

Poha Berry Beef Kebabs ❤

Hands On: 25 minutes
Unsupervised: 5 minutes

1 tablespoon milled black
    pepper*

1 1/4 pounds beef tenderloin,
    stew cut

2 cups cubed pineapple*

3 cups sliced green bell
    peppers

12 cherry tomatoes

12 fresh button mush-
    rooms

1/2 cup poha berry*
    preserves

2 tablespoons cider vinegar

1 tablespoon grated
    ginger*

Heat grill or broiler.

Put cracked peppercorns in bowl and press beef into peppercorns, covering evenly. Alternately place beef, pineapple, and bell peppers on 6 skewers with tomatoes and mushrooms on each end.

Mix in small bowl, preserves, vinegar, and ginger. Brush kebabs with preserve mixture.

Place skewers on hot grill or broiler. Turn once or twice during cooking and brush with more preserve mixture. Cooking time is about 8 to 10 minutes. Serve immediately after cooking.

**Approximate Nutrient
Content per Serving**

Calories	270
Fat	8 g
Saturated Fat	3 g
Cholesterol	60 mg
Sodium	70 mg
Carbohydrate	31 g
Protein	22 g

Always remove skewers before serving to children

Ginger-Pepper Beef ♥

³/₄ pound lean flank steak

¹/₂ cup sherry

2 teaspoons cornstarch

1 teaspoon oyster sauce*

1 clove garlic, minced

1 teaspoon grated ginger*

2 large ripe papayas* (2 pounds each)

2 medium green bell pepper

4 seconds vegetable oil spray

2 tablespoons julienned ginger*

1¹/₂ cup beef broth

1 tablespoon soy sauce

1 tablespoon sugar

1 tablespoon lime juice

¹/₄ cup sliced water chestnuts*

1 cup sliced mushrooms

Approximate Nutrient Content per Serving

Calories	220
Fat	6 g
Saturated Fat	2.5 g
Cholesterol	35 mg
Sodium	510 mg
Carbohydrate	21 g
Protein	17 g

Trim all fat from flank steak. Slice into thin strips across the grain.

Combine sherry, cornstarch, oyster sauce, garlic, and ginger. Marinate beef for 15 minutes.

Meanwhile, peel and seed papayas and cut into 25¹/₂-inch slices. Set aside in refrigerator until needed. Cut bell peppers into thin strips.

Spray wok with vegetable oil spray. Stir-fry beef and ginger for 2 minutes. Add broth, soy sauce, and sugar. Lower heat to medium. Add peppers, lime juice, water chestnuts, and mushrooms. Simmer 5 to 7 minutes.

To serve, arrange 5 slices of papayas fanned out on each plate. Place ¹/₅ of peppered beef in each plate. Serve hot.

Cool fresh sweet papaya compliments the tang of the ginger and peppers.

Thai Beef with Lemon Grass and Thai Basil ♥

3 cups cooked white rice

1/2 pound flank steak

3 seconds vegetable oil spray

3 cloves garlic, minced

1 teaspoon grated ginger*

2 kaffir lime leaves*

1 cup sliced mushrooms

3 tablespoons chopped lemon grass*

1/2 cup beef broth

1/2 cup julienned carrots

2 tablespoons oyster sauce*

1 teaspoon hot chili paste*

10 Thai basil leaves

Trim all fat from beef. Cut into 1-inch thin strips against the grain.

Spray wok with vegetable oil spray. Stir-fry garlic, ginger, beef, kaffir leaves, mushrooms, and lemon grass. Add broth and simmer for 3 minutes. Add carrots, oyster sauce, and chili paste. Simmer for 5 minutes. Remove from heat. Stir in 10 basil leaves. Cover for 2 minutes.

To serve, make rice mound on individual plates and spoon beef over mound. Serve hot.

Approximate Nutrient Content per Serving

Calories	360
Fat	8 g
Saturated Fat	3 g
Cholesterol	45 mg
Sodium	200 mg
Carbohydrate	48 g
	23 g

Thai cooking is fairly simple. Like the Chinese style of cooking, stir-frying is quick. The flavor of kaffir lime, lemon grass and Thai basil is really wonderful.

Beef Broccoli with Oyster Sauce

Makes 4 Servings

Hands On: 15 minutes
Unsupervised: 15 minutes

1 pound top round beef

1 tablespoon soy sauce

2 teaspoons chopped garlic

2 teaspoons chopped ginger*

2 teaspoons cornstarch

2 teaspoons sugar

3 seconds vegetable oil spray

1/2 cup julienned onions

1 1/2 cup beef broth

3 tablespoons oyster sauce*

3 cups broccoli florets and stems

1/2 cup sliced bamboo shoots

1 cup canned straw mushrooms

1 tablespoon cornstarch

1 tablespoon water

Approximate Nutrient Content per Serving

Calories	230
Fat	5 g
Saturated Fat	1.5 g
Cholesterol	65 mg
Sodium	840 mg
Carbohydrate	15 g
Protein	32 g

Trim all fat from meat, cut into thin 1-inch slices against the grain.

Combine soy sauce, garlic, ginger, cornstarch, and sugar. Add beef and marinate for 15 minutes.

Lightly spray wok with vegetable oil spray. Stir-fry onions until soft. Add marinated beef, stir-fry for 4 minutes. Add broth and oyster sauce, stir-fry until sauce is smooth (about 5 minutes). Add broccoli, bamboo shoots and mushrooms. Stir-fry for 3 minutes.

Combine cornstarch and water and add to sauce. Heat until sauce thickens. Serve hot.

Broccoli stalks are as tasty as florets. To make stalks more tender, cut off florets and peel the skin off the stalks. Then cut the stalk in half lengthwise and then cut into thin slices.

Beef Tomato

Hands On: 20 minutes
Unsupervised: 20 minutes

I pound flank steak

5 teaspoons reduced sodium soy sauce

2 tablespoons water

I egg white

I tablespoon cornstarch

2 cloves garlic, minced

$\frac{1}{2}$ cup diced onion

2 cups diced green bell pepper

$\frac{1}{4}$ cup fat-free, reduced sodium chicken broth

I teaspoon sugar

$3\frac{1}{2}$ cups diced tomatoes

$\frac{1}{2}$ cup sliced green onions

$\frac{1}{8}$ teaspoon sesame seed oil

$\frac{1}{8}$ teaspoon toasted sesame seeds

Trim all fat from meat, cut into thin 1-inch slices against the grain.

Combine 2 teaspoons soy sauce plus water, egg white, cornstarch, and garlic. Add beef and marinate for 20 minutes.

Heat wok, add beef and stir-fry for 2 to 3 minutes. Remove beef and drain liquid from wok.

Reheat wok, add onions and pepper and stir-fry for 2 minutes. Return beef to wok. Add remaining soy sauce, broth, and sugar and heat for 1 minute. Add tomatoes, stir, and pour onto hot plates.

Garnish with green onions and sprinkle a few drops of sesame seed oil and sesame seeds on each serving.

Approximate Nutrient Content per Serving

Calories	140
Fat	5 g
Saturated Fat	2 g
Cholesterol	30 mg
Sodium	180 mg
Carbohydrate	11 g
Protein	14 g

This dry sautéing process uses the marinade rather than oil.

Stuffed Cabbage

Makes 5 Servings

Hands On: 15 minutes
Unsupervised: 1 hour

1 large head cabbage
$^1/_2$ pound ground round beef
$^1/_2$ cup diced onions
$^1/_2$ cup diced carrots
4 cloves garlic, chopped
1 teaspoon grated ginger*
1$^1/_2$ cups cooked rice, cold
2 tablespoons chopped
   cilantro*
$^1/_2$ cup plum sauce*
1 tablespoon hoisin sauce*
$^1/_4$ cup chopped green onions
$^1/_2$ cup julienned kamaboko*
$^1/_2$ cup beef broth
1 cup canned diced tomatoes

Remove core from cabbage. Boil water in large stockpot. Place cabbage into boiling water and cook for 10 minutes. Drain cabbage and set aside to cool.

Cook beef in non-stick skillet until no longer pink (about 5 minutes). Pour beef into colander and drain fat. In same skillet, sauté onions, carrots, garlic, and ginger until tender. Add beef to skillet and sauté until beef browns. Add rice and heat thoroughly. Add cilantro, plum sauce, hoisin sauce, green onions, and kamaboko. Remove from heat. Mix well. Cool slightly.

Preheat oven to 350 degrees F.

Carefully remove cabbage leaves to prevent tearing. Divide beef-rice mixture into 5 portions. Spoon mixture onto leaf and roll fairly tight. Tuck edges of cabbage in as it is rolled. Repeat using all mixture.

Place seam side of rolls down in baking dish and pour broth over rolls. Cover with diced tomatoes and any remaining cabbage. Cover baking dish with aluminum foil or baking paper and bake for 45 minutes.

To serve, gently remove rolls from baking dish and drizzle a little diced tomato and beef broth over cabbage. Serve hot.

Approximate Nutrient Content per Serving

Calories	310
Fat	9 g
Saturated Fat	3.5 g
Cholesterol	40 mg
Sodium	750 mg
Carbohydrate	42 g
Protein	17 g

This is a perfect example of cultural culinary blended flavor.

Paniolo Beef
Braised in Beer ❤

Makes 6 Servings

Hands On: 20 minutes
Unsupervised: 1 hour

4 1/2 cups of cooked white
   rice

2 pounds round tip beef,
   stew cut

1 teaspoon salt

1 teaspoon milled black
   pepper*

1/4 cup all-purpose flour

5 seconds vegetable spray

1 cup diced onions

2 teaspoons chopped garlic

2 cups beer

1 cup diced green bell
   pepper

1 cup button mushrooms

1 cup diced tomatoes

Prepare rice.

Season meat with salt and pepper and dust
in flour.

Spray heavy pot (i.e. cast iron or braiser) with
vegetable oil spray. Bring heat to medium high
and sear all sides (about 8 minutes).

Add onions and garlic, sauté until onions are
tender (about 5 minutes). Add beer and simmer
on low heat for 1 hour.

Add bell peppers and mushrooms and simmer for 5 minutes. Add tomatoes and simmer 5
more minutes.

Serve over 3/4 cup hot rice per person.

Approximate Nutrient Content per Serving

Calories	480
Fat	7 g
Saturated Fat	2 g
Cholesterol	85 mg
Sodium	440 mg
Carbohydrate	56 g
Protein	40 g

Paniolos are normally meat and rice eaters,
so this could be their better choice for a
healthy diet.*

Vegetarian Dishes

So, you've invited that big client over to dinner, only to learn that she is a vegetarian! What to cook? This section has vegetarian options with such wonderful flavors that even your client's meat-eater husband will not miss the meat.

There are many other reasons we decided to include vegetarian dishes in this book. These dishes are among our most favorite meals. Nutritionally, even those who have not selected a vegetarian style of eating, can benefit from including vegetarian meals in their overall plan of eating. And health aside, these dishes add a great deal of variety to the flavors in our diets.

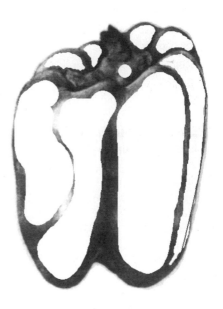

Vegetable Envelopes with Sweet Sour Sauce

Makes 4 Servings

Hands On: 20 minutes

1 ¹/₃ cups Sweet and Sour Sauce (page 191)

1 ¹/₂ cups long rice* (bean thread)

3 seconds vegetable oil spray

¹/₂ cup minced carrots

¹/₂ cup minced zucchini

¹/₄ cup minced celery

¹/₄ cup minced green onions

¹/₄ cup chopped shiitake mushrooms*

2 tablespoons grated ginger*

6 ²/₃ ounces firm tofu, broken in pea size pieces

2 tablespoons hoisin sauce*

¹/₂ teaspoon garlic salt

12 sheets (8 to 10-inch) dried rice paper*

4 pieces ti leaf, 3 x 2-inches

1 cup diced pineapple*

Prepare Sweet and Sour Sauce.

To reconstitute bean thread, soak for 5 minutes in 5 cups hot water. Drain. Cut into 1-inch pieces. Spray wok lightly with vegetable oil spray. Add all vegetables and stir-fry for 3 minutes. Add long rice, tofu, hoisin sauce, and garlic salt, stir-fry for 5 minutes. Remove from wok and cool slightly.

Dampen rice paper with water, When paper is pliable, spoon about ¹/₂ cup of stir-fry vegetables in center. Flatten slightly and fold like an envelope, wrapping fairly snug and secure edges.

Place ti leaf on edge of plate. Overlap 3 vegetable envelopes, spoon 2 tablespoons diced pineapples at base of envelopes and ladle ¹/₃ cup sweet and sour sauce at edge of pineapples.

Serve immediately to prevent envelopes from drying.

Approximate Nutrient Content per Serving

Calories	590
Fat	8 g
Saturated Fat	1 g
Cholesterol	0 mg
Sodium	740 mg
Carbohydrate	118 g
Protein	18 g

An easy way to evenly dampen dried rice paper is with a spray bottle of water.

Yaki Soba with 7 Vegetables

Makes 2 Servings

Hands On: 30 minutes
Unsupervised: 5 minutes

2 teaspoons canola oil

10 ounces refrigerated raw yaki soba noodles*

$1/_2$ cup thinly sliced carrots

$1/_2$ cup thinly sliced jicama*

$1/_2$ cup thinly sliced green beans

$1/_2$ cup thinly sliced red bell peppers

$1/_2$ cup thinly sliced mushrooms

$1/_2$ cup thinly sliced celery

$1/_2$ cup thinly sliced onions

I cup pineapple* juice

2 tablespoons soy sauce

I tablespoon cornstarch

I teaspoon grated ginger*

I tablespoon chopped cilantro*

Add 1 teaspoon oil to wok. Stir-fry noodles, then divide onto 2 plates. Shape the noodles into a ring with an open center.

Heat second teaspoon oil in wok and stir-fry all vegetables in order listed for 3 to 4 minutes.

In a bowl, combine pineapple juice, soy sauce, cornstarch, and ginger. Mix well. Add pineapple mixture to wok, stir-fry until sauce thickens and coats vegetables. Divide vegetable mixture into each noodle ring. Garnish with cilantro. Serve hot.

Approximate Nutrient Content per Serving

Calories	340
Fat	5 g
Saturated Fat	0 g
Cholesterol	0 mg
Sodium	1060 mg
Carbohydrate	66 g
Protein	12 g

For this recipe, grate the ginger instead of chopping it. Method of processing makes a difference to the flavor.

Vegetarian Chow Mein ❤

Makes 4 Servings

Hands On: 25 minutes
3 seconds vegetable spray

1 cup sliced onions

$1/_2$ cup sliced carrots

2 teaspoons chopped garlic

1 cup vegetable broth

2 tablespoons reduced sodium soy sauce

1 tablespoon sherry

1 pound refrigerated raw chow mein noodles

1 can (12 ounces) straw mushrooms, drained and rinsed

2 teaspoons sesame seed oil

1 tablespoon cornstarch

1 tablespoon water

2 cups bean sprouts*

$1/_4$ cup chopped cilantro*

Lightly spray wok with vegetable oil spray. Heat wok and stir-fry onions, carrots, and garlic for 3 minutes. Add broth, soy sauce, and sherry, simmer for 3 minutes. Add noodles, mushrooms, and sesame seed oil and stir-fry for 4 minutes.

Blend cornstarch and water and add to wok. Increase heat to high. Turning ingredients until sauce thickens and coats everything evenly.

Add bean sprouts and cilantro. Stir-fry for 2 minutes to heat thoroughly.

Serve hot.

Approximate Nutrient Content per Serving

Calories	250
Fat	4.5 g
Saturated Fat	0 g
Cholesterol	0 mg
Sodium	1120 mg
Carbohydrate	44 g
Protein	5 g

It is important to use chow mein noodles found in the refrigerator section of the market. Dried chow mein noodles are coated with oil prior to packaging and are exceptionally high in fat.

Choi Sum with Oyster Sauce ♥

Makes 4 Servings

Hands On: 15 minutes

10 ounces dried Thai noodles*

1/2 cup vegetable broth

3/4 cup thinly sliced carrots

1/4 cup chopped green onions

2 teaspoons peanut oil

3 cloves garlic, chopped

3 pounds choi sum*, cut 2-inch lengths

1 teaspoon Chinese yellow bean sauce

2 teaspoons vegetarian oyster sauce

1/2 teaspoon hot chili paste*

In a medium pot, combine vegetable broth and noodles, heat to a simmer. Add sliced carrots and simmer 5 minutes. Add chopped green onions and simmer 7 minutes.

Heat oil in wok, stir-fry garlic for 1 minute. Add choi sum, yellow bean sauce, vegetarian oyster sauce, and chili paste. Stir-fry for 2 minutes or until choi sum softens.

Place noodle on plate and top with choi sum. **Serve** immediately.

Approximate Nutrient Content per Serving

Calories	330
Fat	3 g
Saturated Fat	0 g
Cholesterol	0 mg
Sodium	580 mg
Carbohydrate	69 g
Protein	8 g

This dish really works with any type of cabbage. Each will give a slightly different taste.

Tofu And Eggplant
with Yellow Bean Sauce ♥

2¼ cups cooked Jasmine
  Rice (page 190)

1 teaspoon peanut oil

3 cloves garlic, chopped

1 teaspoon hot chili paste*

4 cups sliced Japanese
  eggplant*

2 tablespoons Chinese
  yellow bean sauce

¼ cup vegetable broth

10 ounces firm tofu*,
  drained and sliced

10 fresh Thai basil leaves

Prepare rice.

Heat oil in wok and stir-fry garlic for 1 minute. Add chili paste and eggplant and stir-fry for 2 minutes.

Add yellow bean sauce and vegetable broth and blend evenly. Gently fold in tofu. Heat thoroughly.

Just before serving, fold basil leaves into mixture.

Serve over ¾ cup jasmine rice per person.

**Approximate Nutrient
Content per Serving**

Calories	400
Fat	11 g
Saturated Fat	1.5 g
Cholesterol	0 mg
Sodium	300 mg
Carbohydrate	58 g
Protein	21 g

Using chili paste is a convenience. Hot chili peppers, fresh or dried can be substituted for the chili paste to meet your "hot" spice preference.

Basque Garbanzo Stew ♥

Makes 3 Servings

Hands On: 15 minutes
Unsupervised: 10 minutes

2 teaspoons olive oil

1 cup chopped onions

1 teaspoon minced garlic

1 teaspoon curry powder

1 teaspoon cumin

$^1/_2$ teaspoon hot chili paste*

1 tablespoon all-purpose
flour

1$^1/_4$ cup vegetable broth

1 cup diced carrots

1 cup diced red potatoes

1 cup diced Granny Smith
apples

1 can (15 ounces) garbanzo
beans, rinsed and drained

1 cup plain low-fat yogurt

2 tablespoons chopped dried
dates

$^1/_8$ teaspoon cinnamon

1 tablespoon chopped
cilantro*

Heat oil in skillet, sauté onions until tender and golden brown. Add garlic, curry, and cumin and sauté for 2 minutes. Blend in chili paste and flour. Cook for 1 minute.

Slowly add and blend broth until smooth and creamy. Add carrots and potatoes and simmer for 5 minutes. Add apples and beans and simmer for 5 more minutes. Remove from heat.

Stir in yogurt until well blended.

In wide-mount shallow soup bowls, ladle stew and garnish with dates, cinnamon, and cilantro. Serve immediately.

**Approximate Nutrient
Content per Serving**

Calories	340
Fat	7 g
Saturated Fat	1.5 g
Cholesterol	5 mg
Sodium	540 mg
Carbohydrate	57 g
Protein	13 g

Basque, the region of Spain bordering France, has a unique blend of flavors dating back to their Spanish-Moorish history.

Mediterranean Lentil Entree Salad ❤

Makes 4 Servings

Hands On: 30 minutes
Unsupervised: 2¼ hours

2 cups brown lentils

4 cups water

4 cloves garlic (2 smashed, 2 minced)

2 teaspoon lime zest*

1 cup diced tomatoes

1 cup diced cucumber

¾ cup diced red onion

½ cup chopped parsley

¼ cup sliced black olives

2 teaspoon capers*

2 teaspoons olive oil

2 tablespoon lime juice

¼ teaspoon milled black pepper*

2 tablespoons chopped basil

½ cup grated low-fat mozzarella cheese

2 whole wheat pita bread

3 seconds vegetable oil spray

4 leaves red Boston lettuce

Approximate Nutrient Content per Serving

Calories	460
Fat	8 g
Saturated Fat	2.5 g
Cholesterol	10 mg
Sodium	340 mg
Carbohydrate	71 g
Protein	30 g

Put lentils and water in stock pot. Add smashed garlic, lemon, and lime zest and bring to a boil. Turn heat down and simmer until lentils are just tender (5 to 10 minutes). Drain lentils. Discard water and smashed garlic. Allow lentils to cool in refrigerator.

In a large bowl, combine minced garlic, tomatoes, cucumber, onions, parsley, olives, capers, olive oil, juices, black pepper, basil, and cheese. Mix well. Add chilled lentils to mixture in bowl. Fold gently.

Preheat oven to 350 degrees F.

Cut pita bread into 6 triangle pieces. Spray lightly with vegetable oil and place on baking sheet. Toast bread until crisp, about 10 minutes.

Place lettuce on chilled plate. Spoon chilled lentil mixture on lettuce and garnish the rim with pita triangles.

This salad is not only low in fat and Calories—it's also inexpensive.

Couscous Marseilles with Spinach, Mushroom and Walnuts ♥

Makes 6 Servings

Hands On: 20 minutes
Unsupervised: 30 minutes

1 1/2 cups couscous*

1/2 teaspoon salt

2 1/2 cups water

3 thin lemon slices

2 teaspoons peanut oil

1/2 cup sliced mushrooms

2 pounds fresh spinach

1/4 cup coarse chopped
   walnuts

1/2 cup diced dried dates

1 teaspoon chopped garlic

2 teaspoons fresh lemon
   juice

1/2 teaspoon salt

1/4 teaspoon black pepper

Spread couscous on large platter. Combine salt and water and sprinkle over couscous. Rub grains to loosen with fingertips. Allow to sit at room temperature for 15 minutes. Line top of steamer with damp cheese cloth. Evenly spread couscous on cheese cloth. Place lemon slices over couscous and cover with cheese cloth edges. Steam for 15 minutes.

Add oil into large skillet and add mushrooms and spinach. Stir fry until spinach wilts (about 2 minutes). Add walnuts and dried dates.

Blend garlic and lemon juice, add mixture to spinach. Cover and simmer for 5 minutes. Season with salt and pepper.

To serve, discard lemon slices on couscous. Fluff couscous and spoon into 4 dishes and shape into a ring. Spoon spinach into center and serve immediately.

Approximate Nutrient Content per Serving

Calories	290
Fat	5 g
Saturated Fat	0.5 g
Cholesterol	0 mg
Sodium	450 mg
Carbohydrate	52 g
Protein	10 g

Do not presoak dried dates, but rather add them in their dry state. This adds a great deal of variety to the texture.

Diamond Head Ratatouille

Makes 6 Servings

Hands On: 20 minutes
Unsupervised: 20 minutes

Soft Polenta (next page)

1 teaspoon butter

1 thinly sliced onion

1 large round diced
eggplant

1 pound trimmed button
mushrooms

5 cloves garlic, minced

1 cup dry white wine or $^{2}/_{3}$
cup vinegar

1 small can diced tomato

$^{1}/_{2}$ teaspoon salt

$^{1}/_{2}$ teaspoon milled black
pepper*

2 tablespoons chopped
fresh basil

Heat butter in heavy skillet. Sauté onions until tender. Add eggplant and sauté 5 minutes. Add mushrooms to onions and garlic. Sauté 5 minutes. Add wine and bring to a boil, then simmer for 5 minutes. Add tomato, stir, cover, and simmer for 10 minutes.

Meanwhile prepare Soft Polenta. Set aside.

Spoon polenta on dish and make a crater in the center.

Season Ratatouille with salt and pepper and spoon into polenta crater and sprinkle with basil. Serve hot.

**Approximate Nutrient
Content per Serving**

Calories	310
Fat	5 g
Saturated Fat	1.5 g
Cholesterol	5 mg
Sodium	1150 mg
Carbohydrate	53 g
Protein	8 g

When washing mushrooms, remember that a mushroom is like a sponge. It absorbs water and releases it during cooking, thus diluting the flavor of the dish. To clean, dampen clean cloth with white vinegar and wipe the mushrooms.

Soft Polenta

6 cups water

1 teaspoon salt

1 1/2 cups yellow cornmeal

1 teaspoon butter

1/2 teaspoon salt

1/4 teaspoon white pepper

Bring water and salt to a boil in a heavy sauce pan. Very slowly add polenta to boiling water, stirring constantly. After all the polenta has been added, continue to cook on low heat and stirring until mixture is thick (about 10 minutes).

Add butter and seasoning. Stir.

From pot, spoon hot polenta on plates and serve.

Approximate Nutrient Content per Serving

Calories	140
Fat	2 g
Saturated Fat	0.5 g
Cholesterol	0 mg
Sodium	550 mg
Carbohydrate	27 g
Protein	3 g

Eastern Indian Saffron Rice ♥ Makes 3 Servings

Hands On: 35 minutes
Unsupervised: 20 minutes

1 cup basmati* rice

1/3 cup split pink lentils

2 1/2 cup boiling water

1 tablespoon canola oil

1/2 cup chopped onions

2 cloves garlic, sliced thin

2-inch piece of fresh
   ginger*

1 cinnamon stick

6 cloves

6 cardamoms*

1/2 teaspoon saffron
   threads*

3/4 teaspoon salt

1/4 cup raisins

Wash rice and lentils. Drain and set aside.

Place saffron in a small container with 1/2 cup of boiling water and set aside.

Heat oil in sauté pan and cook onions until tender. Add garlic and sauté for 2 minutes.

Slice ginger and add it to onions. Sauté for 2 more minutes. Then, add cinnamon, cloves, and cardamoms. Sauté to release spice flavors (2 to 5 minutes).

Add rice and lentils and mix with onions. Add 2 cups boiling water, saffron, and the water from soaking saffron. Stir in salt. Bring pan to a boil, then lower heat, cover pan and simmer for 20 minutes.

Gently fluff rice and add raisins.

Approximate Nutrient Content per Serving

Calories	370
Fat	4 g
Saturated Fat	0.5 g
Cholesterol	0 mg
Sodium	540 mg
Carbohydrate	74 g
Protein	12 g

This recipe can be used as a side dish or a main dish depending on the serving size.

Black-Eye Pea Calcutta ❤

Makes 3 Servings

Hands On: 25 minutes
Unsupervised: overnight

1 cup dried black-eye peas

1 teaspoon canola oil

1 cup thinly sliced onions

2 cloves garlic

1-inch piece fresh ginger*,
    cut in thin strips

1 dried whole red chili

1 teaspoon cumin

1 teaspoon ground
    coriander

1 teaspoon chili powder

$^1/_2$ teaspoon ground
    turmeric*

1 teaspoon black pepper

1 tablespoon tomato puree

$^1/_4$ cup lemon juice

2 tablespoons Madeira
    wine

2 tablespoons chopped
    cilantro*

1 teaspoon salt

Approximate Nutrient Content per Serving

Calories	260
Fat	3 g
Saturated Fat	0 g
Cholesterol	0 mg
Sodium	400 mg
Carbohydrate	44 g
Protein	15 g

Wash beans, cover with water and soak in refrigerator overnight.

Drain beans, place in pot, cover with water and boil for 45 minutes until beans are cooked. Remove from heat and set aside.

Heat oil in large skillet, sauté onions and garlic until tender. Add ginger and chili, then add cumin, coriander, turmeric, and pepper and sauté for 2 minutes.

Drain beans and add to skillet, mixing well. Add tomato puree and simmer for 10 to 12 minutes. Add lemon juice, wine, cilantro, and salt and fold together. Serve hot.

Canned black-eye peas can be used to eliminate soaking and boiling time. Using canned beans, even when rinsed, will increase the sodium for this curry dish.

Eggplant Tamarind ♥

Hands On: 20 minutes
Unsupervised: 2¼ hours

3 cups cooked Brown Rice
(page 189)

1 teaspoon canola oil

1½ pounds long eggplant,
cubed

1 cup thinly sliced onions

2 cloves sliced garlic

1½ teaspoon chili powder

2 teaspoons ground coriander

2 teaspoons turmeric

2 teaspoons mustard seeds

2 bay leaves

¼ cup sliced fresh coconut*

⅛ cup tamarind concentrate

1 tablespoon honey

1 teaspoon salt

1½ teaspoon garam masala

2 Serrano* chilies, ¼-inch
slices

**Approximate Nutrient
Content per Serving**

Calories	300
Fat	6 g
Saturated Fat	2 g
Cholesterol	0 mg
Sodium	590 mg
Carbohydrate	60 g
	7 g

In a large non-stick skillet, heat ½ teaspoon oil and sauté eggplant for 3 minutes. Remove from skillet.

Heat ½ teaspoon oil and sauté onions and garlic until tender. Add chili powder, coriander, turmeric, and mustard seeds. Stir and cook for 2 minutes.

Add bay leaves, coconut, and tamarind concentrate. Stir in honey and add eggplant. Mix well. Season with salt, lower heat, cover and simmer for 10 minutes. Sprinkle garam masala and chilies over mixture and stir to blend evenly. If mixture is too dry or sticks, add a few tablespoons of water to bring back moisture. Low simmer for 5 more minutes.

Serve with ¾ cup steamed rice per person.

Tamarind concentrate can be made from seeds by pouring boiling water over tamarind and soaking for 2 hours. Squeeze tamarind pulp and discard seeds.

Okra and Carrot Curry

Makes 2 Servings

Hands On: 30 minutes
Unsupervised: 5 minutes

1 teaspoon canola oil

1 cup thinly sliced onions

2 cloves garlic, sliced

1 cup thinly sliced carrots

2 teaspoons ground
   coriander

1 teaspoon turmeric

1 teaspoon chili powder

1 teaspoon garam masala

$1/_4$ cup tomato puree

$2/_3$ cup apple juice

4 cups sliced okra

$1/_2$ teaspoon salt

Heat oil in skillet and sauté onions and garlic until tender.

Add carrots and sauté for 2 minutes. Add coriander, tumeric, chili powder, and garam masala and stir. Cook for 2 minutes.

Blend in tomato puree and apple juice, then gently mix in okra and salt and cook on low heat. (Note: This is a dry curry. If the dish is too dry, add a little water to prevent okra from sticking.)

Cover skillet and simmer gently for 5 minutes.

Serve hot.

Approximate Nutrient Content per Serving

Calories	220
Fat	3.5 g
Saturated Fat	0 g
Cholesterol	0 mg
Sodium	720 mg
Carbohydrate	43 g
Protein	7 g

When using fresh okra, be careful not to rub your eyes. The tiny fibers on the okra can cause an irritation to the eyes if rubbed inadvertently.

Spicy Chili James Brian

Makes 10 Servings

Hands On: 25 minutes
Unsupervised: 15 minutes

4 cups vegetable broth

1 cup textured vegetable protein

3 seconds vegetable oil spray

4 cloves garlic, chopped

1 cup chopped onions

$^1/_2$ cup diced celery

1 cup diced green bell peppers

2 teaspoons taco seasoning

1 can (24 ounces) diced tomatoes

1 can (14 ounces) garbanzo beans

1 can (14 ounces) black beans

1 can (14 ounces) kidney beans

2 tablespoons chopped cilantro*

In a large pot, bring broth to boil, add textured vegetable protein and simmer for 10 minutes.

Meanwhile, spray vegetable oil spray into skillet and sauté onions and garlic until tender. Add carrots, celery, and pepper and sauté for 4 minutes. Add taco seasoning. Sauté for 2 minutes.

Add sautéed vegetables to pot containing textured vegetable protein. Mix together. Add tomatoes, garbanzo beans, and kidney beans to textured vegetable protein, cover and simmer for 10 minutes. Add black beans and simmer for 5 minutes. Serve hot and garnish with cilantro.

Approximate Nutrient Content per Serving

Calories	190
Fat	1.5 g
Saturated Fat	0 g
Cholesterol	0 mg
Sodium	890 mg
Carbohydrate	34 g
Protein	12 g

Texture vegetable protein (TVP) comes in many shapes from little granules to 1 to 2-inch strips. TVP takes on the taste of the flavors around it and the texture of meat. TVP can be found in health food stores and some grocery stores.

Stuffed Chayote with Mushroom and Tomato ♥

Makes 4 Servings

Hands On: 15 minutes
Unsupervised: 35 minutes

1 1/2 cups cooked white rice

2 large chayote* (approximately 1 pound each)

2 teaspoons butter

2 cloves garlic, chopped

3/4 cup diced onions

2 cups sliced mushrooms

1 cup diced water-bottled artichoke hearts

1 cup diced fresh tomatoes

3/4 teaspoon salt

1/2 teaspoon white pepper

1/4 cup parmesan cheese

1 teaspoon paprika

2 teaspoons chopped parsley

Preheat oven to 375 degrees F.

Cut chayotes in half. Simmer in water for 20 minutes or until tender. Drain and turn cut side of chayotes on paper towel to drain.

Melt butter in sauté pan, sauté garlic and onions until onions begin to turn golden. Add mushrooms and sauté for 3 minutes.

Meanwhile, scoop out pulp from chayote using a spoon, leave about 1/2-inch of pulp to the skin so the shell will hold its shape. Dice pulp and add to onion-mushrooms mixture, along with artichokes, rice, and tomatoes. Season with salt and pepper. Sauté for 3 minutes.

Fill chayote shells with mushroom mixture. Combine cheese, paprika, and parsley. Sprinkle over filled shells.

Place shells in baking dish and bake uncovered for 15 minutes or until cheese begins to brown. Serve hot.

Approximate Nutrient Content per Serving

Calories	230
Fat	5 g
Saturated Fat	2.5 g
Cholesterol	10 mg
Sodium	590 mg
Carbohydrate	42 g
Protein	9 g

Any summer squash can be used for this dish.

Spaghetti Squash Ticker Tape Parade ♥

Makes 6 Servings

Hands On: 20 minutes
Unsupervised: 15 minutes

1 ½ pounds spaghetti squash

1 teaspoon olive oil

½ cup diced onions

1 teaspoon chopped garlic

¼ cup orange juice

1 cup sliced carrot

1 cup corn kernels

½ cup diced red bell peppers

1 cup frozen peas

1 tablespoon chopped fresh basil

½ teaspoon salt

¼ teaspoon white pepper

¼ teaspoon nutmeg

Quarter lengthwise the squash. Then in a large pot, steam spaghetti squash until tender. Set aside and cool.

Heat oil in large sauté pan. Sauté onions and garlic until very tender and turning slightly golden.

Add orange juice, carrots, and corn and simmer for 5 minutes.

Meanwhile, with a fork scrape the spaghetti-like strands from the squash. Add squash to sauté pan and then combine all remaining ingredients. Sauté for 5 minutes and serve hot.

Approximate Nutrient Content per Serving

Calories	110
Fat	1.5 g
Saturated Fat	0 g
Cholesterol	0 mg
Sodium	240 mg
Carbohydrate	22 g
Protein	3 g

This dish resembles the confetti and streamers of a Wall Street ticker tape parade. It is definitely fun.

Desserts

When a decision is made to eat a healthier diet, a common misconception is that the desserts have to go. Not true! There is nothing wrong with desserts if they are the right ones. Just as there are low-fat soups, salads, appetizers and entrees, it is possible to create low-fat nutrient-rich desserts.

We believe in reality. Most of us crave a dessert now and then. The desserts on the following pages are sweet indulgences that actually help balance your overall diet with healthy low-fat dessert alternatives.

So, when your brain's "dessert center" sends out a cry for goodies, try some desserts with character. Try the cookie bars, brownies, frozen desserts, tortes, or puddings that follow. They are all exceptionally tasty and easy to prepare.

Some of the desserts are award winners and you will not believe by tasting them that they are low-fat. You will learn Chef Pat's and Chef Al's secrets, like how to achieve getting a natural looking blush in a blushing pear, or how to incorporate a traditional staple like breadfruit* into a decadent, yet healthy, dessert.

First we all need to eat to survive. With that accomplished, the second step is to eat to live! Low-fat eating is a big part of the second step. Who can live without desserts and truly be happy? These desserts make it easy to eat and live!

Chocolate-Macadamia Nut Biscotti

Makes 24 Servings

Hands On: 30 minutes
Baking Time: 35 minutes

½ cup chopped unsalted roasted macadamia nuts*

2½ cups flour and ¼ cup for work surface

½ cup cocoa powder

⅛ teaspoon salt

½ teaspoon baking soda

1 teaspoon baking powder

2 eggs plus 1 egg (beaten) for brushing dough

½ teaspoon vanilla

1¼ cups sugar

Preheat oven to 350 degrees F.

Combine nuts, flour, cocoa powder, salt, baking soda, and baking powder in a large bowl. Set aside.

Whisk 2 eggs and vanilla. Add sugar and whisk until sugar dissolves. Slowly add flour mixture, stirring until a soft dough is formed. Divide dough in half.

Lightly flour surface and with flour-dusted hands, roll dough into a cylinder about 2-inches in diameter, 12 to 15-inches long. Repeat with second half. Line baking pan with parchment paper and place rolled dough on top. Brush top of dough with beaten egg.

Bake for 15 minutes or until firm to touch. Remove from oven and gently transfer to cutting board. Cut dough into 12 diagonal slices per roll. Return slices to baking sheet, standing them on edge. Carefully place in oven. Bake until dry and crispy (about 20 minutes).

Cool completely before serving. Store in air-tight container.

Approximate Nutrient Content per Serving

Calories	130
Fat	3 g
Saturated Fat	0.5 g
Cholesterol	25 mg
Sodium	65 mg
Carbohydrate	23 g
Protein	3 g

Biscotti should properly be eaten dipped into coffee, hot chocolate, milk or as the Italians do, dipped in a glass of grappa or sweet wine after dinner.*

Lemon Bars

Makes 9 Servings

Hands On: 15 minutes
Unsupervised: 35 minutes

³/₄ cup all-purpose flour

¹/₄ cup yellow cornmeal

¹/₈ teaspoon salt

¹/₄ teaspoon baking soda

2 tablespoons applesauce

¹/₃ cup sugar

3 eggs (1 egg yolk and
  white separated)

1 tablespoon plain nonfat
  yogurt

¹/₂ teaspoon vanilla extract

3 seconds vegetable oil
  spray

¹/₂ cup sugar

¹/₂ cup lemon juice

1 tablespoon lemon zest*

¹/₄ cup all-purpose flour

1 tablespoon powdered
  sugar

Approximate Nutrient Content per Serving

Calories	170
Fat	2 g
Saturated Fat	0.5 g
Cholesterol	70 mg
Sodium	90 mg
Carbohydrate	35 g
Protein	4 g

Preheat oven to 350 degrees F.

In a medium bowl, mix flour, cornmeal, salt, and baking soda. Set aside.

In a second medium bowl, whip applesauce and sugar until sugar dissolves. Whisk 1 yolk, yogurt, and vanilla into applesauce mixture.

Add flour mixture to applesauce mixture and mix well. Knead slightly to blend ingredients evenly. Press dough lightly into an 8-inch square pan sprayed with vegetable oil spray. Prick dough with fork. Bake for 20 minutes or until golden brown.

While cookie dough is baking, prepare topping. Whip 2 eggs (and remaining egg white from yolk in cookie crust). Whisk in lemon juice, zest and flour. Mix until smooth. When cookie crust is brown, lower oven to 300 degrees F, pour lemon topping over hot cookie crust and bake for 15 to 18 minutes.

Remove from oven, cool on rack and chill until topping completely sets.

To serve, cut into 2-inch squares and dust with powdered sugar. (This recipe does not freeze well.)

Lemon bars typically are outrageously high in fat. Chef Pat developed this recipe so that we can still enjoy lemon bars without the guilt.

Chocolate Zucchini Brownie with Triple Berry Sauce ❤

Makes 20 Servings

Hands On: 20 minutes
Unsupervised: 35 minutes

3¼ cups Triple Berry Sauce (page 198)

3½ cups whole wheat flour

½ cup cocoa powder

1 teaspoon cinnamon

1 teaspoon baking soda

¼ teaspoon baking powder

2 cups sugar

¾ cup egg substitute

½ cup prune paste

½ cup applesauce

1 teaspoon vanilla extract

2½ cups finely shredded zucchini

8 seconds vegetable oil spray

¼ cup powdered sugar

Prepare Triple Berry Sauce.

Preheat oven to 350 degrees F.

Sift flour, cocoa, cinnamon, baking soda, and baking powder in a medium bowl. Set aside.

In a large bowl, beat sugar, egg substitute, prune paste and applesauce. Add vanilla. Fold in zucchini and then gradually fold in flour mixture.

Prepare 2 sheet pans with spray (4 seconds each). Divide the batter between the 2 pans and bake for 20 to 25 minutes. Cool completely.

Sprinkle with powdered sugar, cut and serve with 2½ tablespoons of Triple Berry Sauce.

Approximate Nutrient Content per Serving

Calories	220
Fat	1 g
Saturated Fat	0 g
Cholesterol	0 mg
Sodium	90 mg
Carbohydrate	51 g
Protein	5 g

This brownie, developed by Chef Pat, was grand prize winner for the 1996 Low-Fat Cooking Challenge at the Great Aloha Run's Health and Fitness Expo. It is also on the cover of the Honolulu Magazine's 1996 Honolulu Restaurant Guide. Using whole wheat flour gives a chewy brownie, using cake flour makes it more cake-like.

Apricot Almond Taro Cakes   Makes 12 Servings

Hands On: 20 minutes
Baking Time: 30 minutes

¹/₂ cup pureed apricot baby
    food

¹/₂ cup granulated sugar

I teaspoon almond extract

2 egg whites

³/₄ cup enriched white flour

³/₄ cup taro*flour

I teaspoon baking powder

¹/₂ cup ground almonds

¹/₂ cup apricot jam

Preheat oven to 350 degrees F.

Cream apricot puree with sugar. Add extract and egg whites. Beat well.

Sift flour, taro flour and baking powder in a separate bowl. Stir in almonds. Add flour mixture to apricot mixture and work into a stiff paste.

Line a 9-inch square baking pan with parchment paper. Press half of the paste mixture evenly on the bottom of the pan. Spread thin layer of apricot jam over paste mixture. Spread remaining paste over jam.

Bake for 30 minutes. Cool and cut into 12 pieces.

**Approximate Nutrient
Content per Serving**

Calories	160
Fat	3 g
Saturated Fat	0 g
Cholesterol	0 mg
Sodium	55 mg
Carbohydrate	31 g
Protein	4 g

Taro flour is generally located in the baking section of the grocery store.

Orange Ice Grand Marnier ♥   Makes 4 Servings

Hands On: 20 minutes
Chill Time: 4 hours

4 oranges (nice in appearance)

1 ½ cups orange sorbet*

1 tablespoon Grand Marnier

4 tablespoons light cool whip topping

4 maraschino cherries

½ tablespoon minced macadamia nuts*

4 mint leaves

Remove tops from oranges and completely scoop out orange pulp. Mince and reserve ½ cup orange pulp. Freeze empty orange shells.

In a medium bowl, combine orange pulp, sorbet, and Grand Marnier. Mix well.

Fill empty orange shells with sorbet mixture and freeze until firm (2 to 4 hours).

Before serving, garnish with topping, macadamia nuts, cherry, and mint.

Approximate Nutrient Content per Serving

Calories	130
Fat	1.5 g
Saturated Fat	0.5 g
Cholesterol	0 mg
Sodium	15 mg
Carbohydrate	28 g
Protein	1 g

This is a recipe Chef Al created in 1965 and served as the finale for hundreds of fine dinners. The Grand Marnier can be eliminated if a non-alcoholic version is desired.

Nectarine and Wine Sherbet ♥

Makes 12 Servings

Hands On: 25 minutes
Unsupervised: 24 hours

1¼ cups Pastry Cream
(page 197)

4 cups peeled and sliced
nectarines plus 12 slices
fresh ripe nectarines

2 cups water

²/₃ cup chablis wine

1 cup sugar

²/₃ cup plain nonfat yogurt

4 teaspoons Just Whites®
meringue powder

¼ cup warm water

Prepare Pastry Cream.

In a sauce pot, cook nectarines with water. When fruit is tender, drain water and puree nectarines.

Return the puree to sauce pot and add wine and sugar. Heat mixture and stir until sugar dissolves. Boil for 2 minutes. Remove from heat and cool slightly. Blend in yogurt and pour into ice cube trays and freeze until slushy.

Whisk meringue powder with warm water until stiff but not dry. Fold meringue gently into semi-frozen sherbet, blend evenly and place in covered container. Return to freezer and freeze until firm.

Serve with pastry cream and sliced nectarines.

Approximate Nutrient Content per Serving

Calories	140
Fat	0 g
Saturated Fat	0 g
Cholesterol	0 mg
Sodium	35 mg
Carbohydrate	31 g
Protein	3 g

An ice cream machine could also be used to make this dessert.

Blushing Pears with Raspberry Sorbet ❤

Makes 4 Servings

Hands On: 15 minutes
Unsupervised: 30 minutes

4 Seckle pears

1 cup cranraspberry juice concentrate

1 cup white wine

1 cinnamon stick

4 cloves

²/₃ cup brown sugar

1 orange peel

1 cup sliced strawberries

1¹/₃ cup banana slices

1 kiwi*, diced

1 cup raspberry sorbet*

Peel and core pears.

In a medium-size sauce pot, combine juice, wine, cinnamon, cloves, sugar, and orange peel. Simmer for 10 minutes. Gently add pears into liquid and simmer for 15 to 20 minutes. Pears should be tender but still firm. Remove from liquid and allow to cool for 4 -5 minutes at room temperature.

Gently combine strawberries, banana, and kiwi.

Place 1 warm pear with ¹/₄ cup sorbet and ¹/₄ fruit mixture. Serve immediately. Note: Any variety of pear may be used if seckle pear is not available. Cooking time of pear will vary depending on size and firmness of the pear.

Approximate Nutrient Content per Serving

Calories	360
Fat	1 g
Saturated Fat	0 g
Cholesterol	0 mg
Sodium	40 mg
Carbohydrate	81 g
Protein	2 g

Chef Pat created this recipe in 1983. Instead of using a red wine to get the blushing color, which sometimes overwhelms the delicate flavor of the pear, Chef Pat created this cranberry juice and white wine combination. The pear has a true inner pastel pink blush. This dessert was televised in 1991 on Pamela Young's Mixed Plate, "Romantic Dinner for Two." Even if you do not care for pears, you will like them served this way.

Lychee Ginger Sorbet* ♥

Hands On: 25 minutes
Unsupervised: 4 hours

$^1/_4$ cup sugar

$1^1/_2$ cups water

2 tablespoons chopped
lemon grass*

1 tablespoon ginger juice*

$4^1/_2$ cups pureed ripe
lychees*

Heat sugar, water, and lemon grass in sauce pan. Simmer for 10 minutes. Strain into medium size freezable bowl. Discard lemon grass. Add ginger juice and lychee puree and mix well. Cover bowl and freeze.

After 45, 65, and 85 minutes, remove from freezer and whisk. After whisking the third time, the texture should be loose and have light frozen bits. Return to freezer and freeze for at least 2 hours before serving.

**Approximate Nutrient
Content per Serving**

Calories	120
Fat	0 g
Saturated Fat	0 g
Cholesterol	0 mg
Sodium	0 mg
Carbohydrate	31 g
Protein	1 g

This is a perfect ending to a great meal. It is very light and fresh. The ingredients are not over powering, but compliment the natural lychee sweetness.

Warm Chocolate Pudding Parfait ♥

3 tablespoons cocoa
  powder

2 1/2 teaspoon cornstarch

1 cup skim milk

1 egg yolk

3 tablespoons sugar

1/2 teaspoon vanilla extract

1 1/3 cup vanilla nonfat
  frozen yogurt

Combine cocoa and cornstarch in small sauce pan, gradually add milk, stir and bring to a boil, stirring constantly. Cook for 1 minute and remove from heat.

In a small bowl, whisk egg yolk and sugar together. Add 1/2 cup warm milk mixture.

Slowly pour egg mixture into remaining milk in sauce pan while whisking constantly. Stir over medium-low heat until thickened (about 7 minutes). Remove from heat, add vanilla extract and cool slightly.

Spoon 1/4 cup warm pudding into parfait glass. Top with 1/3 cup nonfat frozen yogurt. Top with 2 more teaspoons of warm pudding drizzled over frozen yogurt. Serve immediately.

Approximate Nutrient Content per Serving

Calories	170
Fat	2 g
Saturated Fat	1 g
Cholesterol	55 mg
Sodium	95 mg
Carbohydrate	33 g
Protein	8 g

This dessert is better than a hot fudge sundae and a favorite of the classes presented by Fish & Poi Chefs. This dessert was televised on Filipino Beat's 1996 Holiday Meals.

Pistachio Rice Pudding with Rose Water ♥

Makes 4 Servings

Hands On: 15 minutes
Unsupervised: 1 1/2 hours

1/4 cup calrose or short grain rice

2 cups water

2 inches stick of cinnamon

4 cloves

4 cups skim milk

1/2 cup light brown sugar

4 whole cardamon seeds

1/4 cup raisins

1/8 cup chopped pistachio nuts

1/2 teaspoon rose water

Wash rice well. Place in pot and cover with 2 cups of water. Bring to a boil and add cinnamon and cloves. Boil for 20 minutes. Rice should be fully soft. Pour out excess water.

Add milk and bring to a simmer. Add sugar and cardamon and continue to simmer until mixture is thick (about 45 minutes). Stir in raisins and pistachios and cover pot. Heat on very low for 30 minutes. Remove from heat.

Sprinkle rose water over pudding. Spoon into serving dishes and refrigerate before serving.

Approximate Nutrient Content per Serving

Calories	280
Fat	2.5 g
Saturated Fat	0.5 g
Cholesterol	5 mg
Sodium	140 mg
Carbohydrate	55 g
Protein	10 g

Chef Pat learned a lot of Indian cooking as the Personal Chef for Doris Duke. This is an Indian rice pudding called Khir that Pat converted to low-fat.

Bread Pudding with Mandarin Orange Sauce ♥

Makes 24 Servings

Hands On: 20 minutes
Unsupervised: 70 minutes

Mandarin Orange Sauce
Recipe (next page)

2½ cups sugar

4½ cups evaporated skim
milk

12 egg whites only

1 cup raisins

2 cups tart apples

2 teaspoons vanilla extract

2 teaspoons cinnamon

1 teaspoon nutmeg

1 loaf (1 pound) French
bread

4 seconds vegetable oil
spray

Prepare Mandarin Orange Sauce.

Preheat oven to 350 degrees F.

Heat sugar and milk just enough to dissolve sugar (about 10 minutes). Stir in egg whites and then, raisins, apples, vanilla, cinnamon and nutmeg. Remove from heat. Set aside.

Slice French bread into thin slices. Arrange bread in baking pan. Pour egg mixture over the top of the bread. Make sure that raisins and apples fall between slices. Press gently on top of bread to absorb liquid. Set aside for 10 minutes.

Spray the top of the bread with vegetable oil spray. Bake for about 1 hour.

Pour 2½ tablespoons sauce over each serving of pudding just before serving.

**Approximate Nutrient
Content per Serving**

Calories	240
Fat	1 g
Saturated Fat	0 g
Cholesterol	0 mg
Sodium	220 mg
Carbohydrate	51 g
Protein	9 g

In place of 12 egg whites, you can use 1⅔ cups of fat-free egg substitute.

Mandarin Orange Sauce ♥

Makes 4 Cups

$^1/_3$ cup fresh orange juice

2 cups plain nonfat yogurt

1 cup mandarin oranges

$^1/_3$ cup honey

$^1/_3$ cup lemon juice

1 teaspoon lemon zest*

1 cup peeled and minced apple

Place orange juice, yogurt, mandarin oranges, honey, lemon juice, zest, and apple in blender and blend until smooth. Pour sauce over pudding before serving.

Approximate Nutrient Content per 2 Tablespoons

Calories	25
Fat	0 g
Saturated Fat	0 g
Cholesterol	0 mg
Sodium	10 mg
Carbohydrate	5 g
Protein	1 g

This sauce is great on many desserts.

Peach and Apple Crisp á la Mode ❤

Hands On: 15 minutes
Unsupervised: 40 minutes

3 seconds vegetable oil spray

2 cups thinly sliced green apples

2 cups sliced peaches

3 1/2 tablespoons dark brown sugar

1/8 teaspoon fresh grated nutmeg

1 tablespoon cornstarch

1 tablespoon skim evaporated milk

1/2 cup all-purpose flour

1/2 cup rolled oats

1/2 cup granulated sugar

1/2 teaspoon baking powder

1/4 teaspoon cinnamon

2 teaspoons applesauce

2 cup nonfat frozen yogurt

Preheat oven to 375 degrees F.

Lightly spray 8-inch square baking dish. Add apples, peaches, brown sugar, nutmeg, cornstarch, and milk. Mix ingredients well and spread evenly.

Combine flour, oats, sugar, baking powder, and cinnamon. Fold in applesauce. Sprinkle over apple mixture.

Bake until golden brown (about 35 minutes). Top this warm dessert with 1/4 cup of frozen yogurt.

Approximate Nutrient Content per Serving

Calories	210
Fat	1 g
Saturated Fat	0 g
Cholesterol	0 mg
Sodium	70 mg
Carbohydrate	47 g
Protein	5 g

This is a comfort food that will never lose it's popularity.

Breadfruit (Ulu) á la Mode ♥

Makes 8 Servings

Hands On: 10 minutes
Unsupervised: 1 1/2 hours

1 medium ripe breadfruit*, about 6-inches in diameter

1 quart water

1/2 cup applesauce

1 tablespoon apricot preserve

1/2 teaspoon pumpkin spice

1 teaspoon brown sugar

1 lemon

1 teaspoon lemon zest*

2 cup nonfat frozen yogurt

In a medium stockpot, combine water and add whole breadfruit. Bring to a boil, then simmer for 75 minutes. Turn breadfruit occasionally for even cooking. Remove breadfruit from water and allow to cool slightly.

Cut breadfruit in half lengthwise. Remove the core from center.

Combine applesauce and apricot preserve and fill the breadfruit. Sprinkle pumpkin spice and brown sugar over top and squeeze lemon juice over breadfruit. Sprinkle top with lemon zest.

Place each breadfruit half facing up in baking pan and bake in preheated oven for 15 minutes. Slice each half into 4 wedges and serve warm with 1/4 cup of nonfat frozen yogurt.

Approximate Nutrient Content per Serving

Calories	160
Fat	0 g
Saturated Fat	0 g
Cholesterol	0 mg
Sodium	25 mg
Carbohydrate	40 g
Protein	3 g

Chef Al created this great tasting low-fat version of this ulu dessert.

Apple Strudel ♥

Makes 8 Servings

Hands On: 15 minutes
Unsupervised: 40 minutes

8 cups sliced Granny Smith apples

3 tablespoons dark brown sugar

1 tablespoon flour

2 tablespoons orange juice

1 teaspoon ground allspice

8 seconds vegetable oil spray

6 phyllo dough sheets

1/2 cup dried bread crumbs

2 teaspoons powdered sugar

Preheat oven to 350 degrees F.

In large bowl combine apples, brown sugar, flour, orange juice, and allspice. Mix well.

Lightly spray phyllo sheets with vegetable oil spray (1 second each), sprinkle with 2 teaspoons bread crumbs, lay second sheet, spray and sprinkle with bread crumbs. Continue this process until all 6 sheets are stacked together evenly.

Spread apples over phyllo leaving a 1½-inch edge boarder. Roll up strudel starting from the long side jelly rolled style. Press ends together. Place seam side down on baking sheet pan. Spray with vegetable oil spray (2 seconds).

Bake until golden brown (35 to 40 minutes). Remove from oven and sift powdered sugar over the top.

Cut into 8 pieces. Serve warm or at room temperature.

Approximate Nutrient Content per Serving

Calories	170
Fat	2.5 g
Saturated Fat	0 g
Cholesterol	0 mg
Sodium	125 mg
Carbohydrate	36 g
Protein	2 g

This is a family favorite. There are as many variations of strudels as there are pastry chefs. This is a very simple version and of course low-fat.

Mango, Cranberry, Apple and Cherry Cobbler ♥

Makes 16 Servings

Hands On: 15 minutes
Unsupervised: 45 minutes

6 cups sliced green tart apples

¹/₂ cup dried cranberries

4¹/₂ cups sliced mango*

1 can (16 ounces) pitted Bing cherries, drained

1 cup apple juice concentrate

1 cup applesauce

2 teaspoons cinnamon

1 teaspoon nutmeg

¹/₂ cup honey

¹/₂ cup cornstarch

3 egg whites

1 cup whole wheat flour

¹/₂ cup rolled oats

¹/₂ cup brown sugar

¹/₄ cup applesauce

¹/₄ cup apple juice concentrate

Preheated oven to 375 degree F.

In a glass baking dish (8 x 12 x 2-inch) combine apples, cranberries, mangoes, cherries, apple juice, applesauce, cinnamon, nutmeg, honey, and cornstarch. Mix ingredients well and set aside.

In a mixing bowl, whip egg whites until foamy, about 2 minutes. Add flour, roll oats, brown sugar, applesauce and apple juice. Mix well.

With fingers, crumble dough on top of fruit mixture in glass baking dish. Bake until top should be golden brown (about 45 minutes). Serve hot for best results.

Approximate Nutrient Content per Serving

Calories	240
Fat	1 g
Saturated Fat	0 g
Cholesterol	0 mg
Sodium	20 mg
Carbohydrate	59 g
Protein	3 g

Cobblers can be made with any fruit, but fresh fruits taste best. In this recipe, dried cranberries add a chewy texture. Raisins can substitute for cranberries.

Watermelon Chiffon 4th of July ♥

Hands On: 20 minutes
Unsupervised: 60 minutes

3 cups watermelon juice

1/3 cup sugar

1/8 teaspoon salt

2 envelopes unflavored gelatin

1 tablespoon lime juice

1/8 teaspoon cream of tartar

4 teaspoons Just Whites® meringue powder

1/4 cup warm water

2 tablespoons sugar

1/2 cup Lite Cool Whip®

2 cups watermelon balls

1/4 cup chopped almonds

Cut off and discard melon rind. Cube melon and remove seeds. Place melon in blender and puree. Place a fine mesh strainer over a bowl and strain watermelon liquid. Discard pulp. You will need 3 cups of watermelon juice.

In a sauce pot, add sugar and salt to juice and stir. Sprinkle gelatin over juice, stir and let sit for 5 minutes to soften gelatin. Now place sauce pot over medium heat until gelatin and sugar are completely dissolved, stirring the whole time. Add lime juice and stir. Remove from heat, place in a large bowl and refrigerate for 1 hour.

Whisk meringue powder with warm water, sugar, and cream of tartar until they form and hold a peak and then fold into chilled watermelon mixture. Fold in 1/2 cup whip into mixture.

Refrigerate until chiffon is firm, at least 6 hours. Decorate with watermelon balls and chopped almonds just before serving.

Approximate Nutrient Content per Serving

Calories	120
Fat	3 g
Saturated Fat	1 g
Cholesterol	0 mg
Sodium	50 mg
Carbohydrate	20 g
Protein	4 g

A watermelon dessert with no seeds. Freeze excess watermelon juice during the summer and have the sweetness of summer-picked watermelons all year round.

Baked Apples with Mincemeat en Phyllo ♥

Makes 4 Servings

Hands On: 20 minutes
Unsupervised: 25 minutes

1 teaspoon cinnamon

2 teaspoons granulated sugar

4 medium Granny Smith
apples

2 cups water

$1/2$ lemon, juice only

$1/2$ cup canned mincemeat*

2 sheets (14 x 18-inch)
phyllo dough*

6 seconds butter-flavored
vegetable oil spray

4 tablespoons low-fat
cheddar cheese

Preheat oven to 350 degrees F.

Combine cinnamon and sugar. Mix well and set aside.

Peel and core apples. Set in water and lemon juice for a few minutes. Drain apples and fill apple centers with 2 tablespoons mincemeat. Sprinkle with cinnamon-sugar mixture.

Spread out 2 phyllo sheets and cut in quarters. Cover with damp towel to prevent drying.

Place 1 phyllo quarter on flat surface and spray phyllo dough lightly with butter-flavored oil spray (1 second). Place a second quarter of phyllo criss-cross the first. Place an apple in the center of sheets and top with 1 tablespoon cheddar cheese. Pull the phyllo around each apple making a phyllo pouch. Spray the outside of the phyllo lightly with butter-flavored oil spray. Bake for 20 to 25 minutes.

**Approximate Nutrient
Content per Serving**

Calories	210
Fat	3 g
Saturated Fat	0 g
Cholesterol	0 mg
Sodium	190 mg
Carbohydrate	45 g
Protein	2 g

Why settle for ordinary baked apples, when you can have this! Even without the phyllo dough, this dessert is a treat.

Pumpkin-Pineapple Upside Down Cake ♥

Makes 12 Servings

Hands On: 10 minutes
Unsupervised: 45 minutes

6 seconds butter flavored oil spray

2 tablespoons apricot puree

²/₃ cup brown sugar

1¹/₂ cups drained crushed pineapple*

15 pitted red cherries

15 pitted prunes

1 box Betty Crocker™ Lemon Sweet Rewards cake mix

¹/₃ cup applesauce

2 tablespoons prune paste

1 cup canned pumpkin

6 egg whites

¹/₄ cup chopped walnuts

¹/₂ cup water

2 tablespoons rum (optional)

Preheat oven to 375 degrees F.

Lightly spray sides and bottom of 13 x 9 x 2-inch high baking pan with butter flavoring.

Spread apricot puree evenly on bottom of pan. Then spread brown sugar, crushed pineapple, cherries and prunes.

In a bowl, mix the cake mix, applesauce, prune paste, pumpkin, egg whites, walnuts and ¹/₂ cup water. Mix for 2 to 3 minutes.

Pour cake batter over pineapple mixture in pan. Bake for about 45 minutes.

When cake is done, remove from oven and cool on rack for about 10 minutes. Place a rectangle tray over pan and invert cake onto tray. Sprinkle with rum.

Approximate Nutrient Content per Serving

Calories	280
Fat	2.5 g
Saturated Fat	0 g
Cholesterol	0 mg
Sodium	250 mg
Carbohydrate	58 g
Protein	4 g

This recipe is easy and as close to mistake proof as you can get.

Chocolate Strawberry Torte ♥ Makes 12 Servings

Hands On: 15 minutes
Unsupervised: 40 minutes

3¹/₂ cups cake flour

¹/₂ cup cocoa powder

1 teaspoon cinnamon

1 teaspoon baking soda

¹/₄ teaspoon baking powder

2 cups sugar

3 eggs

1 cup applesauce

1 teaspoon vanilla extract

2¹/₂ cups finely shredded
zucchini

8 seconds non-stick
vegetable spray

¹/₂ cup apricot jam

1 tablespoon fresh lime
juice

2 teaspoon lime zest*

2¹/₂ cups Lite Cool Whip®
Topping

2 cups sliced strawberries

2 teaspoons cocoa powder

Preheat oven to 350 degrees F.

Sift flour, cocoa, cinnamon, baking soda and baking powder in a medium bowl.

In a large bowl, beat sugar, eggs, applesauce, and vanilla. Fold in zucchini and gradually fold in flour mixture.

Prepare 2 cake pan (8-inch) with spray. Divide the batter between the pans and bake for 20 to 25 minutes. Cool completely.

Meanwhile, puree jam, lime juice, and zest. Spread thinly over top of each cake.

Layer 1 cup sliced strawberries and cover with second cake. Layer top of cake with Cool Whip and remaining strawberries in center. Sprinkle of cocoa powder on outer edge of Lite Cool Whip®.

Approximate Nutrient Content per Serving

Calories	350
Total Fat	3 g
Saturated Fat	2 g
Cholesterol	0 mg
Sodium	150 mg
Carbohydrate	76 g
Protein	7 g

This is our cake version of the Chocolate Zucchini Brownie.

Chocolate Amaretto Souffle Torte with Raspberries ♥

Makes 10 Servings

Hands On: 15 minutes
Unsupervised: 35 minutes

2 seconds vegetable oil spray

1/4 cup Grapenuts® cereal

3 tablespoons all-purpose flour

1 tablespoon semi-sweet chocolate chips

1/2 cup unsweetened cocoa powder

1 cup sugar

1/2 cup boiling water

1 egg yolk

2 tablespoons amaretto liqueur

4 egg whites, room temperature

1/4 teaspoon cream of tartar

2 teaspoons powdered sugar

1 1/2 cups Pastry Cream (page 197)

1 cup fresh raspberries

Preheat oven to 375 degrees F. Place a round parchment paper into the bottom of an 8-inch springform pan (about 3-inches deep). Spray vegetable oil spray on the sides of pan.

Place cereal and flour in food processor and grind until very fine. Set aside.

In a large mixing bowl, combine chips, cocoa and 3/4 cup of sugar. Add boiling water and whisk until chocolate melts and mixture is smooth. Whisk in egg yolks and amaretto. Set aside.

Beat egg whites and cream of tartar until soft peaks form. Gradually add remaining 1/4 cup sugar and beat at high speed until stiff but not dry. Set aside.

Whisk cereal mixture into chocolate mixture. Fold in 1/4 of egg white, then gently fold in remaining egg whites. Gently scrape batter into springform pan.

Bake for 30 to 35 minutes. Remove from oven and cool on rack. Torte will drop like a souffle. After torte has cooled, run a knife between torte and sides of pan to free torte. Invert torte on a plate, remove pan and paper liner, then turn right side up on another plate or cakeboard circle.

To serve, sprinkle lightly with powdered sugar, cut into 10 slices, place on a plate, drizzle 2 tablespoons pastry cream on plate and scatter raspberries on plate and serve.

Because this torte is flat and sunken when done, even a novice can feel successful. This torte can be served at room temperature 1 hour to 1 day later.

Approximate Nutrient Content per Serving

Calories	210
Fat	2 g
Saturated Fat	0.5 g
Cholesterol	20 g
Sodium	70 mg
Carbohydrate	45 g
Protein	6 g

Lilikoi Mousse ♥

Hands On: 30 minutes
Unsupervised: 4 hours

2 teaspoons unflavored
    gelatin

3 tablespoons cold water

$^1/_4$ cup concentrated lilikoi*
    juice

$^3/_4$ cup sugar

$^1/_4$ cup fat-free egg substitute

I teaspoon vanilla extract

3 tablespoons Just Whites
    meringue powder®

$^2/_3$ cup warm water

$^1/_2$ teaspoon cream of tartar

$^1/_2$ cup Lite Cool Whip®
    Topping

Sprinkle gelatin over 3 tablespoons cold water in a small cup. Set aside to soften. Do not stir for 5 minutes.

In a sauce pan, combine lilikoi juice and $^1/_4$ cup sugar and simmer.

In a small bowl, whisk 1 tablespoon hot lilikoi mixture with egg substitute. Scrape egg mixture into lilikoi juice and stir constantly on low heat for 3 to 4 minutes. Pour mixture into bowl.

Stir in softened gelatin and vanilla and whisk evenly. Set bowl into large bowl filled with ice. Scrape sides as mixture begins to thicken and set. Remove bowl and set aside.

Whisk meringue powder with warm water and cream of tartar until soft peaks form. Gradually add remaining sugar and beat until stiff but not dry.

Fold lilikoi mixture into meringue and then gently fold in Cool Whip®. Spoon into parfait glasses and chilled for 4 hours.

Approximate Nutrient Content per Serving

Calories	230
Fat	I g
Saturated Fat	I g
Cholesterol	0 mg
Sodium	95 mg
Carbohydrate	45 g
Protein	8 g

This is a very light texture dessert.

Baked Alaska with Triple Berry Sauce ❤

Makes 4 Servings

Hands On: 25 minutes
Unsupervised: 3 ½ hours

½ cup Triple Berry Sauce
(page 198)

4 store bought short cakes

1 ½ cups nonfat frozen
yogurt

8 teaspoons Just Whites®
meringue powder

½ cup warm water

½ teaspoon cream of tartar

½ cup sugar

Prepare Triple Berry Sauce.

Place short cake on baking sheet. Scoop a rounded 3 ounces scoop of frozen yogurt and place it on top of short cake. Place in freezer for 15 minutes.

Whisk meringue powder with warm water, and cream of tartar until they form and hold a soft peak. Gradually add sugar and beat until stiff but not dry peaks.

Fill pastry bag with meringue. Bring 1 shortcake out from freezer. Using a pastry bag, pipe meringue onto shortcake, completely covering cake and frozen yogurt. Carefully return to freezer. Repeat with 3 remaining shortcakes. Freeze for 3 hours.

Preheat oven to 425 degrees F.

Bring 4 meringue shortcakes from freezer on baking pan. Place in preheated oven for 6 to 8 minutes or until meringue is lightly browned. Individual Alaskas could be served or returned to freezer to serve later.

Place on plate with 2 tablespoons Triple Berry Sauce and serve immediately.

Approximate Nutrient Content per Serving

Calories	320
Fat	2 g
Saturated Fat	0.5 g
Cholesterol	15 mg
Sodium	240 mg
Carbohydrate	67 g
Protein	10 g

Because of the growing problem with salmonella in eggs, a processed egg white product, called Just Whites®, is used. Pleasure without the concern.

Basic Recipes

Several basic recipes used throughout this book are provided in this section. We call them basic since they do not have all the frills. However, they can add wonderful depth to a recipe.

Broth or stock, what's the difference? Some of our recipes include the ingredients chicken broth, fish broth, and vegetable broth. We use the term "broth" to refer to a what you can buy in a store, usually in a can. The term "stock" refers to what you can make yourself, using fresh ingredients in your own kitchen. The positive side of making your own stock is that you control the flavor and amount of sodium. Store-bought broths are convenient when you're tight on time. But, choose them carefully since most contain considerable amounts of sodium and some are high in fat. Read and compare labels. The nutrient values for the recipes using broth as an ingredient are based on typical sodium values for commercial products. If you make your own stocks with the recipes on the following pages, it can greatly reduce the sodium content of the recipe.

Cooking is an art and a science. We prefer that flavors are balanced and complementary. Nothing on the plate should compete with or overpower something else. When everything is attempting to be a "star," you can't have a winning team. To win an oscar, the entire cast must work together. To produce a winning meal, all of the ingredients must work together.

Have you ever gone out for a meal and someone asked if you liked the meat or the sauce? You answered, "the sauce." Many chefs would take it as a compliment. We believe that a truly satisfied diner would answer, "I like the whole meal." It is like an oscar winning movie. The combination of the entire cast working together brings out the best from each other.

Vegetable Stock

Makes I quart

Hands On: 10 minutes
Unsupervised: 2 hours

3 seconds vegetable oil
   spray
1½ tablespoons chopped
   shallots
1 cup diced leek, white
   part only
1 cup chopped mushrooms
1½ cup diced carrot
1½ cup diced celery
4 parsley stems
2 cups diced tomato
1 bay leaf
1 sprig thyme
1 teaspoon whole black
   peppercorns
1½ quarts water

Spray large stockpot with vegetable oil spray. Sauté ingredients (except water) over medium heat just until tender; not brown.

Add water and bring to a boil. Lower heat and simmer for 1½ to 2 hours.

Strain and discard solids.

Cool and then refrigerate or freeze stock.

**Approximate Nutrient
Content per Cup**

Calories	10
Fat	1 g
Saturated Fat	0 g
Cholesterol	0 mg
Sodium	5 mg
Carbohydrate	0 g
Protein	0 g

Old vegetables will not make a fresh tasting stock. If possible, buy your produce in quantities as you require them.

Chicken Stock

Makes I quart

Hands On: 10 minutes
Unsupervised: 2¼ hours

2 pounds raw chicken
 carcasses, necks, wings,
 giblets, except the liver

2 quarts water

2 cups diced onion

1½ cups diced carrot

1 cup diced celery

2 cups diced leek, white
 part only

1 bay leaf

4 parsley stems

1 sprig thyme

2 teaspoons whole black
 peppercorns

Rinse chicken in cold water. Place chicken and water in large stockpot and bring to a boil. Skim any impurities from surface.

Add remaining ingredients. Bring to a boil, then lower heat to simmer for 2 hours. Periodically skim any impurities from surface.

Strain and discard solids.

Cool and then refrigerate. When cold, skim and discard any visible solid fat.

Use within two days or freeze until needed.

**Approximate Nutrient
Content per Cup**

Calories	10
Fat	0.5 g
Saturated Fat	0 g
Cholesterol	0 mg
Sodium	10 mg
Carbohydrate	0 g
Protein	0.5 g

When freezing stocks, use a tight-sealing container filled 1-inch from the top. Remember to label and date it.

Fish Stock

Hands On: 10 minutes
Unsupervised: 1 hour

2 pounds fish bones, heads, no gills or internal organs

2 cups diced onion

1 cup diced celery

2 cups diced leek, white part only

2 bay leaves

1 teaspoon whole black peppercorns

1 sprig thyme

4 stems parsley

2 cups dry white wine

2 quarts water

1 lemon, cut in half

Rinse bones.

Combine ingredients in large stockpot. Squeeze lemon halves into pot and drop halves into stock. Bring to a boil. Lower heat to simmer for 40 minutes. Periodically skim any impurities from surface.

Strain and discard solids.

Cool and then refrigerate or freeze stock.

Approximate Nutrient Content per Cup

Calories	80
Fat	0 g
Saturated Fat	0 g
Cholesterol	0 mg
Sodium	15 mg
Carbohydrate	1 g
Protein	1 g

Rinsing the fish bones is important both for flavor and appearance of the stock. Never use fish bones older than 24 hours.

Brown Rice ♥

Makes 6 Servings

Hands On: 5 minutes
Unsupervised: 45 minutes

3 cups water
¼ teaspoon salt
1½ cups brown rice

Rice Cooker Method:

Combine all ingredients. Cover and press "Cook" button. Cooking will take 30 to 40 minutes.

When cooked, fluff rice, cover and allow to sit for 5 minutes before serving.

Rangetop Method:

In a 2-quart sauce pan, bring salt and water to a boil. Add rice. Cook for 15 minutes, stirring occasionally. Lower heat to simmer. Place cover on pot and cook until done (about 30 minutes). Fluff rice and let sit 5 minutes before serving.

Approximate Nutrient Content per ¾ Cup

Calories	180
Fat	1.5 g
Saturated Fat	0 g
Cholesterol	0 mg
Sodium	95 mg
Carbohydrate	36 g
Protein	4 g

Salt can be eliminated from this recipe to lower sodium if desired.

Jasmine Rice

Makes 4 Servings

Hands On: 5 minutes
Unsupervised: 45 minutes

1 cup water
1 cup Jasmine rice

Rice Cooker Method:

Combine all ingredients. Cover and press "Cook" button. Cooking will take 30 to 40 minutes.

When cooked, fluff rice, cover and allow to sit for 5 minutes before serving.

Rangetop Method:

In a 2-quart sauce pan, bring water to a boil. Add rice. Cook for 15 minutes, stirring occasionally. Lower heat to simmer. Place cover on pot and cook until done (about 30 minutes). Fluff rice and let sit 5 minutes before serving.

Approximate Nutrient Content per $^3/_4$ Cup

Calories	200
Fat	0 g
Saturated Fat	0 g
Cholesterol	0 mg
Sodium	0 mg
Carbohydrate	43 g
Protein	4 g

Jasmine rice is a medium-grain white rice. This method can be used for any standard white rice, except for quick-cooking types.

Sweet and Sour Sauce

Makes 3 cups

Hands On: 15 minutes

1 tablespoon orange zest*
1 teaspoon lime zest*
1/4 cup orange juice
2 tablespoons lime juice
3 tablespoons grated ginger*
1 cup ketchup
1 cup white granulated sugar
3/4 cup cider vinegar
1 tablespoon cornstarch
1 tablespoon water

Prepare zests.

Squeeze juice of orange and lime in sauce pan. Add ginger, ketchup, sugar, and vinegar. Bring to a boil.

Mix cornstarch and water to make a paste.

Stir paste into other ingredients to thicken. Remove from heat.

Add lime and orange zests.

Approximate Nutrient Content per 2 Tablespoons

Calories	45
Fat	0 g
Saturated Fat	0 g
Cholesterol	0 mg
Sodium	120 mg
Carbohydrate	12 g
Protein	0 g

Use within 48 hours, reheat prior to use.

Marinara Sauce I ♥

Makes 2½ cups

Hands On: 5 minutes
Unsupervised: 30 minutes

1 teaspoon olive oil

1 cup finely diced onion

4 cloves garlic, minced

1 can (28 ounces) peeled
diced plum tomatoes

1 teaspoon fresh chopped
fresh basil

¼ teaspoon salt

In a sauce pan, heat oil and sauté onions until transparent.

Add garlic and sauté for 2 minutes.

Add tomatoes and simmer for about 15 minutes.

Add basil and salt and simmer for 10 minutes. Remove from heat when mixture is a sauce-like consistency.

**Approximate Nutrient
Content per ½ Cup**

Calories	60
Fat	1.5 g
Saturated Fat	0 g
Cholesterol	0 mg
Sodium	370 mg
Carbohydrate	10 g
Protein	2 g

Marinara can be made ahead of time and stored in the refrigerator for 3 days.

Marinara Sauce II ❤

Makes 4 cups

Hands On: 10 minutes
Unsupervised: 25 minutes

3 seconds vegetable oil spray

$^1/_2$ cup finely diced onion

I clove garlic, minced

5$^1/_2$ cups peeled, seeded, and diced ripe tomatoes

I tablespoon chopped fresh basil

$^1/_2$ teaspoon salt

Spray sauce pan with vegetable oil spray. Over a medium heat, sauté onions until transparent.

Add garlic and sauté for 2 minutes.

Add tomatoes and simmer for 12 to 15 minutes.

Add basil and salt and simmer for 5 minutes. Remove from heat when mixture is a sauce-like consistency.

Approximate Nutrient Content per $^1/_2$ Cup

Calories	35
Fat	I g
Saturated Fat	0 g
Cholesterol	0 mg
Sodium	140 mg
Carbohydrate	7 g
Protein	I g

This is a fresher option to Marinara I. Use within 48 hours, reheat prior to use.

Roasted Garlic Paste

Hands On: 3 minutes
Unsupervised: 50 minutes

4 large whole garlic bulbs, do not cut—leave whole

³/₄ cup water

1 tablespoon brandy or white wine

Preheat oven to 350 degrees F.

In a small baking pan, place root-end of whole garlic heads down on a small baking pan. Pour water into the pan and bake in oven for 40 minutes.

Remove from oven and cool slightly.

Cut bottom root-end of garlic and squeeze cloves into food processor. Add brandy and puree until smooth.

Place in a tightly sealed container. Refrigerate until needed.

Approximate Nutrient Content per 2 Tablespoons

Calories	40
Fat	0 g
Saturated Fat	0 g
Cholesterol	0 mg
Sodium	0 mg
Carbohydrate	8 g
Protein	1 g

Brandy or white wine is a great way to preserve the roasted garlic and add flavor to dishes.

Pickled Ginger
(Garni Shoga)

Makes 2 cups

Hands On: 15 minutes
Unsupervised: 60 minutes

1 1/2 cups peeled and thinly
  shaved fresh ginger*

2 cups water

1 3/4 cups rice vinegar*

6 tablespoons sugar

1 teaspoon salt

Rinse ginger in cold running water. Place in boiling water for 1 minute and then rinse in cold water. (Reserve 5 tablespoons boiling water).

Bring water from ginger and vinegar to a boil. Add sugar and salt. Heat until dissolved.

Add ginger to vinegar mixture. Bring to boil and immediately remove from heat. Allow to cool.

Place pickled ginger in clean, airtight jar. Store in refrigerator up to 3 months.

**Approximate Nutrient
Content per 2 Tablespoons**

Calories	20
Fat	0 g
Saturated Fat	0 g
Cholesterol	0 mg
Sodium	110 mg
Carbohydrate	5 g
Protein	0 g

This is excellent for refreshing the palette and waking-up the taste buds.

Chili Pepper Water

Makes 2 cups

Hands On: 5 minutes

5 - 6 smashed Hawaiian chili peppers

$^1/_2$ teaspoon Hawaiian salt

2 cups hot water

In a clean warm small glass bottle, combine chili peppers, salt, and hot water.

Approximate Nutrient Content per Tablespoon

Calories	0
Fat	0 g
Saturated Fat	0 g
Cholesterol	0 mg
Sodium	35 mg
Carbohydrate	0 g
Protein	0 g

Small ketchup bottles are the ideal size for keeping chili pepper water.

Pastry Cream

Hands On: 15 minutes

3 tablespoons sugar

1 1/2 tablespoons flour

1 1/2 tablespoons cornstarch

1 cup skim milk

1/3 cup fat-free egg substitute

1 teaspoon vanilla extract

Combine sugar, flour, and cornstarch in a sauce pot. Add milk and mix well.

Place sauce pot on medium heat. Stirring constantly, cook until milk thickens, then decrease heat to low.

In a small bowl, whisk egg substitute completely. Add 1/4 cup of hot milk mixture into egg and whisk.

Gradually whisk egg mixture into pot with thickened milk. Continue to cook over low heat for 3 minutes, stirring constantly.

Pour custard into clean bowl. Whisk in vanilla extract. Cool, cover, and refrigerate. Use within 24 hours.

Approximate Nutrient Content per 2 Tablespoons

Calories	35
Fat	0 g
Saturated Fat	0 g
Cholesterol	0 mg
Sodium	25 mg
Carbohydrate	6 g
Protein	2 g

This recipe could meet the low-fat guidelines using an egg and an egg yolk. Because the egg in the recipe is not heated enough to destroy bacteria, we choose to use an egg substitute that has been pasteurized.

Triple Berry Sauce ❤

Hands On: 10 minutes
Unsupervised: 20 minutes

2 cups sliced fresh strawberries

2 cups cranraspberry juice

¹/₂ cup sugar

¹/₂ teaspoon lemon extract

¹/₂ teaspoon vanilla extract

Rinse and remove hulls from strawberries. Place in food processor and puree. Set aside.

Combine juice and sugar in medium sauce pot and bring to a boil. Lower heat to simmer for 15 minutes until liquid thickens.

Add strawberry puree to thicken juice. Simmer for 10 minutes. Remove from heat and cool slightly.

Add lemon extract and vanilla extract. Cool sauce and refrigerate. Serve chilled or warm.

**Approximate Nutrient
Content per 2 Tablespoons**

Calories	25
Fat	0 g
Saturated Fat	0 g
Cholesterol	0 mg
Sodium	0 mg
Carbohydrate	7 g
Protein	0 g

The blend of strawberry, cranberry, and raspberry flavors is wonderful and can be used with all types of desserts.

Glossary

Ahi
Hawaiian name for yellowfin or bigeye tuna. Also called shibi in Japanese. Often served raw as sashimi.

Al Dente
Italian phrase meaning to cook pasta until almost soft.

Apple Banana
A small banana (about 4-inches) which has a mild flavoring of apples.

Arborio Rice
A short and fat grain rice grown in Italy that is high in starch, providing a creamy texture to rice dishes.

Balsamic Vinegar
A vinegar made from a white grape juice and aged in wooden barrels for a period of years. It has a very dark color and special soft flavor that is picked up from the wood of the barrels used for aging.

Basmati Rice
A long-grain nut-flavored rice, originated from the Himalayas.

Bean Sprouts
Usually refers to sprouted mung beans, however soy beans, lentils, and sometimes other beans are used in sprouted form. Generally consumed raw or lightly stir-fried.

Bonito Flakes
Dried Tuna shavings.

Bourride
Mediterranean fish soup with garlic, onions, and orange peel.

Breadfruit
Also known as *'ulu* in Hawaiian, native to the Pacific, this large melon-size starchy fruit can be boiled, steamed, baked, broiled, or deep-fried. It is generally consumed as the starchy staple with a meal and can substitute for potatoes when green and firm or for sweet potatoes when ripe and slightly soft.

Cannelloni
Large pasta tubes, generally stuffed with meat or cheese fillings.

Capers
Pickled small flower buds of a bush native to the Mediterranean. Typically, they are rinsed before using to remove excess salt and added to dishes or sauces for their unique pungent flavor.

Cardamon
A strong flavored and aromatic spice from India and found in the tropics. This spice is related to the ginger family.

Char Siu
Marinated Cantonese-style barbecued or roasted pork that is red in color with a sweet and spicy flavor. Commonly used in stir-fry dishes.

Chayote
A large, 1-2 pound, squash-like fruit of a prolific vine native to Central America. It can be used like summer squash in many recipes.

Chili Oil
Vegetable oil flavored with hot chilies. It should be kept in the refrigerator.

Chili Paste
A paste made of fava beans, flour, hot red chilies and possibly garlic. It is used in Chinese cooking.

Chinese Parsley - See Cilantro.

Chocolate Syrup
This syrup is a fat-free source of chocolate flavor, not to be confused with chocolate sauce or chocolate fudge that are usually much higher in fat.

Choi Sum
A green leafy type of Chinese cabbage with tender, mildly flavored leaves.

Chop Suey Vegetables
A mixture of chopped vegetables, generally consisting of mushrooms, bean sprouts, onions, celery, bamboo shoots, and waterchestnuts.

Chow Fun Noodles
Wide, flat rice noodles commonly used in Chinese dishes with vegetables and meat.

Cilantro
Leaves of the coriander plant. Also known as Chinese parsley, it is used commonly in Asian, Indian, Mexican, and Caribbean cooking. It has a pungent odor and flavor that may not appeal to some people.

Coconut
The fruit or nut of the coconut palm. Most commonly available as the meat of the mature nut shredded or flaked.

Coconut Syrup
A syrup made from coconut milk and sugar, and often contains considerable fat.

Couscous
A granular form of semolina typically available in precooked form for quick cooking. Its culinary uses are similar to rice or other mildly flavored grains.

Croutons
Small pieces of bread which have been toasted. These can be plain or seasoned.

Crystallized Ginger
Candied ginger root slices that are coated with coarse sugar crystals. Used as a confection or in desserts.

Curly Endive
A slightly bitter green leafy vegetable used mostly as a salad ingredient. Sometimes mistakenly called chicory in the United States, it grows in open or loose leafy heads with the outer leaves dark green and the inner leaves usually off-white.

Cuttlefish
Similar to squid (calamari) and octopus, it is more tender but still needs to be tenderized. In the dried form, it is usually soaked in water before cooking.

Daikon
A large Asian radish, usually white in color, it is used shredded raw for salads and garnishes or cooked similar to turnips in soups and stir-fry.

Dashi
A Japanese soup stock made from dried bonito tuna flakes, kombu (kelp) and water. Dashi-no-moto is an instant form of this stock.

Enoki Mushroom
Small mushroom with spaghetti-like strands; crunchy in texture.

Fava Beans
Similar to the lima bean, Fava beans are also known as Faba beans or Broad beans

Furikake
A seasoning made from seaweed, sesame seeds, and salt that is used to add flavor and color to rice and noodles.

Garbanzo Beans
This is a tan-colored legume, also called chickpeas.

Ginger
The root of a specific variety of ginger plant that has a pungent, spicy, and peppery hot flavor. It is used as a seasoning both in savory dishes (typically with garlic and soy sauce) and in sweets such as cookies, cakes, and candies.

Ginger Juice
The liquid extracted when ginger is grated and squeezed; juice is strained of fibers.

Grappa
This is a colorless high alcohol distilled beverage, made from grapes.

Guava
A sweet, tangy, and fragrant tropical fruit that is eaten fresh or sweetened and made into a fruit nectar, jam, or jelly. It is commonly available in Hawai'i, California, and Florida. Guava season in Hawai'i is typically "choke" with various varieties of the fruit growing wild in the forests.

Habañero Chili Pepper
A small lantern-shaped chili which is extremely hot.

Hawaiian Chili Pepper
A very small (1/2 to 1 inch long) and very hot red chili pepper.

Hawaiian Sweet Potato - See Purple Sweet Potato.

Hoisin Sauce
A thick reddish-brown fermented soy bean sauce that is seasoned with garlic and chile peppers and used with meats, poultry, shellfish, and stir-fry.

Japanese Eggplant
This smooth-skin fruit is long (6 to 12-inches) and thin (about 1 to 2-inches diameter) and is also known as the Asian eggplant.

Japanese Pear
Also called Asian pear, there are many varieties of this type of pear that is firm and crunchy when ripe. Most are delicately sweet in flavor and quite juicy.

Jicama
A large root vegetable with a thin brown skin and a crunchy sweet white flesh. Can be eaten raw or cooked. Also known as the Mexican potato.

Kabocha Squash
A winter squash with a grayish-green rind and orange flesh that is very tender, smooth, and slightly sweet. It may be used like acorn or butternut squash for baking or steaming and also makes a wonderful ingredient in soups.

Kaffir Lime Leaf
The leaf of the kaffir lime is used to impart a citrus flavor and aroma to many cooked dishes. The leaf is very fibrous so it is not consumed. Sometimes substituted for lemon grass.

Kamaboko
The Japanese word for fish cake made in the form of a cake or loaf of pureed, steamed fish that is pressed or formed into various shapes. The outside layer is most commonly colored pink or red (though other colors exist) with the inside white in color. When sliced, it can be very decorative.

Katsu Sauce
A thick dark spicy sauce made from tomato, sugar, vinegar, apple, salt, carrot, cornstarch, garlic, onion, ginger, and soybeans.

Kiwi
Also called kiwi fruit or Chinese gooseberry, it is slightly bigger than a large chicken egg. Covered with a brown fuzzy coating, the fruit has a brilliant green, sweet, tart, flesh. Peeled and sliced, the fruit makes a decorative garnish. Grown commercially in both New Zealand and California. It is available year-round.

Kombu
Sun-dried sheets of kelp that are used to flavor a variety of cooked foods and sushi. The natural white powder on the surface of the dried seaweed contains much of the flavor.

Lemon Grass

A key ingredient in Thai cooking that adds a lemon flavor and fragrance to soups and other dishes. Since the grass is very fibrous, it is not consumed unless ground into a fine powder. Sometimes substituted for kaffir lime leaves.

Lilikoi - See Passion Fruit

Long Rice

Translucent thread-like noodles made from mung bean flour. Typically they are soaked in water before cooking.

Lychee (also litchi, lichee, litchi nut)

A small (1 to 2-inches in diameter) Chinese fruit with a bright red rough outer shell and a translucent, juicy, sweet, and delicately flavored flesh surrounding a single inner seed. Typically eaten fresh plain or as part of fruit salads. When the fruit is dried in the shell, it may be referred to as a lychee nut, but only the dried fruit portion is edible.

Macadamia Nuts

A rich flavorful nut that is a major crop in Hawai'i. It is consumed fresh or roasted and is used in many forms as a key ingredient in products such as candies, cookies, ice cream, and can be substituted in most any dish that uses nuts. The nut is very high in fat. So, consume in moderation and store refrigerated or frozen to prevent rancidity of the oils.

Mango

A sweet flavorful fruit when ripe, there are many varieties of mango. They range from greenish-yellow to red in color when ripe with yellow to bright orange flesh. The ripe fruit is consumed fresh plain or in fruit salads and is sometimes dried. The tart green mango is used in a variety of Asian and Hawaiian dishes.

Manoa Lettuce

A tender leaved semi-heading lettuce similar to butter lettuce. Also known as Green Mignonette.

Mesclun Greens

A mixture of young, small salad greens.

Milled black pepper

This pepper is freshly ground or cracked. Pre-ground black pepper is considerably stronger in flavor. Cracked black pepper is occasionally available in supermarkets.

Mincemeat
A preserve made of dried fruits, usually apples, apricots, pears, raisins, cherries, candied citrus, nuts, beef suet, spices, and rum or brandy.

Mirin
A sweet golden rice wine used to add sweetness and flavor to many Japanese dishes. If mirin is unavailable, one teaspoon of sugar can be used to substitute for one tablespoon of mirin.

Miso
A Japanese fermented soybean paste, usually high in salt, and used to season soups, main dishes, sauces, marinades, dips, and salad dressings. There are several varieties that range in color from golden-yellow to dark brown, with the darker misos more strongly flavored.

Mochi Rice
Sometimes called sweet rice, this is a short-grain, very glutinous rice.

Mochiko Rice Flour
Flour made from mochi rice.

Monchong
Also known as Bigscale or Sickle Pomfret. This deep water fish has firm white flesh and is generally 4-25 pounds.

Nairagi - Also known as a Striped Marlin or A'u.

Ogo
A type of seaweed used fresh and grown commercially in Hawai'i. Its red filaments have a crisp texture and a slightly salty mild flavor.

Okinawan Sweet Potato - See Purple Sweet Potato.

Onaga - Also known as the Ruby Red Snapper.

Opah - Also known as Moonfish.

Opakapaka - Also known as Crimson Snapper.

Oyster Sauce
A concentrated dark-brown sauce made from oysters, salt, and soy sauce. Used in many Asian dishes to impart a full, rich flavor. Also available in vegetarian forms.

Papaya

Although many varieties of papaya are grown around the world, the most common variety in Hawai'i is a sweet, yellow, pear-shaped fruit, about 6 to 10 inches long. It is a common breakfast fruit in Hawai'i, served sliced in half with the central cluster of seeds removed.

Passion Fruit

Also called lilikoi in Hawaiian, the most common variety of this fruit in Hawai'i has a yellow, shiny outer shell filled inside with seeds surrounded with a juicy pulp. The juice is tangy and unique in flavor, delicious in drinks, sauces, dressings, and desserts.

Pekoe Tea

A specific grade of tea that has medium-sized tea leaves.

Persimmon

A sweet red-orange fruit that is most commonly available in two very different varieties. The Hachiya variety is about the size of a large orange but more elongated in shape. It must be allowed to ripened until soft or the fruit is very astringent. The Fuyu variety is smaller and has the shape of a vertically flattened tomato. The Fuyu can be eaten when still firm and crunchy.

Phyllo Dough

Tissue-thin layers of pastry dough similar to strudel dough. Phyllo is available in many supermarkets in fresh or frozen forms.

Pickled Ginger

Young ginger root sliced thinly and pickled in sweet vinegar. Used as a common Japanese condiment and garnish, typically pink or red in color.

Pineapple

A large (2-5 pounds) pine cone shaped tropical fruit. Sweet and tangy, it is available primarily fresh and canned.

Plum Sauce

This is a thick sweet and sour sauce made from plums, apricots, sugar, and seasonings.

Poha

Also known as cape gooseberry, golden berry, or ground cherry, the yellow, marble-sized fruit hangs on the plant inside a lantern-shaped paper-like "wrapper" (calyx), giving each fruit its own wrapper. It is eaten raw or in jams and pies.

Prickly Pear
The fruit of various varieties of cactus. The skin can be green to purplish-red in color. Somewhat like a melon in flavor, sweet, but rather bland in flavor.

Purple Sweet Potato
Also called Okinawan or Hawaiian sweet potato, this sweet potato has deep purple flesh. This should not be confused with the Peruvian purple potato.

Quinoa
A small grain from Central America that is used much like couscous or rice.

Radicchio
A red-leaf Italian chicory used most commonly in green salads.

Rice Flour
Available as regular rice flour, made from regular white rice and used in baked goods, or as sweet rice flour made from short grain glutinous rice and used for confections, dumplings, or a thickener for sauces.

Rice Paper Wrappers
Thin sheets made from rice flour, water, and salt that are used to wrap around meat, fish, or other mixtures for Thai spring rolls.

Rice Ribbon Noodles
A flat rice noodle commonly used in Thai cooking.

Rice Vinegar
Vinegar made from fermented rice. It is typically milder than most Western vinegars.

Rice Wine
Typically made from steamed glutinous rice, this type of wine is found as various types in Japan such as sake and mirin and in China as chia fan, and yen hung.

Saffron
This is a bright yellow-orange spice which is considered the world's most expensive spice, but is required in tiny amounts.

Sake - See rice wine.

Salmonella

A bacteria found in raw meat and poultry. More recently this bacteria is also found in eggs. Cross-contamination of other foods by Salmonella occurs easily and therefore all cutting boards and knives should be thoroughly cleaned before using with other foods.

Serrano Chile

This small chile (about 2-inch long) has a very hot flavor and is often used in salsas.

Sesame Oil

Oil pressed from the sesame seed is available in two forms. That pressed from the raw seed is light in color and flavor and can be used for a wide variety of purposes. When the oil is pressed from the toasted sesame seed, it is dark in color with a much stronger flavor and is especially common in Korean and Chinese cooking.

Shiitake Mushrooms

Also called black Chinese mushrooms and forest mushrooms, they are used both fresh and dried. The texture is meaty and the flavor is full. Dried shiitake need to be soaked until soft (about 20 minutes). The stems are tough, but can be used to make delicious soup stock.

Shoga - See Pickled Ginger.

Shutome - Also known as Broadbill Swordfish.

Soba

This Japanese noodle is made from buckwheat and wheat flour and is generally brown in color.

Sorbet

Frozen dessert made from fruit juice, pureed pulp, and sugar. Does not contain milk products, but may contain wine, liqueur, or egg whites.

Soy Sauce

A salty liquid made from fermented boiled soybeans and roasted barley or wheat. Usually dark brown in color, it is the principal seasoning in many styles of Asian cooking.

Star Fruit

Also called carambola, this sweet-tart fruit has a five pointed star shape when cut crosswise. Excellent for flavor and decoration.

Taco Seasoning

Blend of Mexican ingredients such as chili, cilantro, onions, peppercorns, garlic in a ground form. Ratio of ingredients varies from one brand to another.

Taro

A starchy tuber which is found in tropical areas and West Africa. This tuber is also grown in some parts of the southern United States. This is the plant used to make Hawaiian poi.

Thai Noodles - See Rice Ribbon Noodles.

Ti Leaves

Large shiny smooth green leaves of the ti plant that are used to wrap a variety of foods for cooking. The leaves are not consumed.

Tofu

Made from curdled soy milk, tofu is usually custard-like in texture (soft tofu), but can be quite firm when more liquid is drained during a process of pressing (regular or firm). It is bland in flavor and will take on the flavors of other foods and seasonings with which it is prepared.

Turmeric

This spice is yellow-orange in color and has a bitter pungent flavor. This spice is used primarily for curries.

Uku - Hawaiian name for Gray Snapper Fish.

Water Chestnuts

Crispy white edible tubers of a water plant that have a brownish-black skin resembling a regular chestnut. Very popular in Asian cooking, water chestnuts are available fresh or canned.

Watercress

A member of the mustard family with crisp dark green leaves that have a slightly bitter and peppery taste. It is used raw in salads and cooked in soups and other dishes.

Wet Lemon Peel

Sweetened and salted lemon rind also known as Chinese lemon preserve.

Wheat Germ

The germ or embryo portion of the wheat grain is a good source of several vitamins, minerals, and protein. It has a nutty flavor and is high in oil content. Its oil can turn rancid quite quickly.

Won Bok

A type of Chinese cabbage sometimes referred to as celery cabbage. It is pale green in color with a broad white stem, somewhat similar to romaine lettuce in shape, with a delicate mild flavor.

Zest

The outer-most skin of citrus contains strongly flavored oils. Zest can be grated or cut into fine strips.

Percent Calories from Protein, Carbohydrate, Fat, and Alcohol and Diabetic Exchanges

Page		Protein	Percent Calories* From Carbohydrate	Fat	Alcohol	Diabetic Exchanges**
	DRINKS AND BEVERAGES					
2	Lemon-Lime Thirst-Quencher	6	90	4	0	Free
3	Chef's Cocktail	1	98	2	0	1.5 Fr
4	Maui Plantation Dazzle	2	98	1	0	2.5 Fr
5	Kona-Sunset Frappé	5	91	3	0	1.5 Fr
6	Physical Workout Spritz	6	85	8	0	1.25 Fr
7	Hawaiian-Honeymooners' Cocktail	4	94	2	0	2.5 Fr
8	Mocha Nog	24	69	7	0	1 Fr, 1 SM
9	Christmas Cranberry Float	1	94	5	0	3.5 Fr
10	Raspbango Tango	3	94	2	0	4 Fr
11	Ikaika's Bionic Strawberry Defense	6	89	4	0	2.5 Fr, 0.5 SM
12	James Brian's Speckled Float	3	92	5	0	2 Fr, 1 St
13	Matson Nectar	3	93	3	0	4 Fr
14	Puna Moon Eclipse	7	85	8	0	3.5 Fr, 0.5 LM
15	Old Homestead Mist	8	86	5	0	2 Fr, 0.5 SM
16	Spark-of-Genius	5	89	7	0	2.5 Fr
17	Mango-Apricot Margarita	1	63	1	34	2 Fr, 1.5 Fat
18	White Lady Froth	6	63	5	27	4 Fr, 1 SM, 2.5 Fat
19	Sangria (Spanish Punch)	5	94	1	0	1.5 Fr

* For ease of use, the percent of Calories from protein, carbohydrate, fat, and alcohol were rounded to use no decimal point, therefore the sum of the percents may occasionally total 99% or 101%.

** For some recipes, diabetic exchange values per serving were adjusted to more closely represent the actual Calorie, carbohydrate, protein, and fat content than strictly food-based exchanges.

Diabetic Exchange Abreviations: Fr=Fruit; LM=Low-fat Milk; SM=Skim Milk; St=Starch; VLMt=Very Lean Meat, LMt=Lean Meat, MMt=Medium-fat Meat, HMt=High-fat Meat; Veg=Vegetable; Other=Other Carbohydrates; Fat=Fat Group; Free=less than 5 grams carbohydrates and 20 Calories.

| Page | | **Percent Calories* From** | | | | Diabetic Exchanges** |
		Protein	Carbohydrate	Fat	Alcohol	
20	Kilauea-Iki Blast	15	74	11	0	2 Veg, 1 Fr
21	Vegetable Perk-Me-Up	15	76	9	0	2 Veg, 1 Other
22	Creamed Field of Greens	33	61	6	0	3 Veg, 1 SM
23	**BREADS**					
24	Cornmeal Muffins with Honey	11	71	18	0	1.5 St, 0.5 Fat
25	Orange-Cranberry Scones	9	79	12	0	1 St, 1 Fr
26	Lemon Tea Bread	10	75	15	0	1 Fr, 0.5 St, 0.5 SM
27	Mango-Banana Bread	8	81	11	0	2 Fr, 1 St
28	Pecan-Topped Pumpkin Bread	5	84	11	0	2.5 Fr, 1 St
29	Apricot Bread	8	86	6	0	1.5 Fr, 1.5 St
30	Boston Brown Bread	9	71	20	0	1 St, 0.5 Fr, 0.5 Fat
31	Bagels	13	80	7	0	2 St, 1 Other
32	Sweet Potato Rolls	12	71	17	0	1.5 St, 0.5 Fat
33	Potato Bread	10	78	11	0	2 St
34	Russian Black Bread	13	77	10	0	2 St, 1 Fr, 1 Veg
35	**STARTERS - APPETIZERS, SOUPS AND SALADS**					
36	Marinated Green Mango Appetizer	11	82	8	0	1.5 Fr, 2 Veg, 0.5 Fat
37	Cilantro Black Bean Dip with Pita Bread	18	77	5	0	2 St, 2 Veg

* For ease of use, the percent of Calories from protein, carbohydrate, fat, and alcohol were rounded to use no decimal point, therefore the sum of the percents may occasionally total 99% or 101%.

** For some recipes, diabetic exchange values per serving were adjusted to more closely represent the actual Calorie, carbohydrate, protein, and fat content than strictly food-based exchanges.

Diabetic Exchange Abbreviations: Fr=Fruit; LM=Low-fat Milk; SM=Skim Milk; St=Starch; VLMt=Very Lean Meat; LMt=Lean Meat; MMt=Medium-fat Meat; HMt=High-fat Meat; Veg=Vegetable; Other=Other Carbohydrates; Fat=Fat Group; Free=less than 5 grams carbohydrate and 20 Calories.

Percent Calories* From

Page		Protein	Carbohydrate	Fat	Alcohol	Diabetic Exchanges**
38	Mushroom Quesadillas with Tomato-Pineapple Cilantro Salsa	14	60	25	0	1 St, 1 Veg
39	Tomato-Pineapple Cilantro Salsa	11	77	12	0	0.25 Veg
40	Crab Cakes with Pink Grapefruit Cream	38	46	16	0	2 VLMt, 1 Veg, 1 Fr, 0.5 Fat
41	Pink Grapefruit Creme	3	95	2	0	Free
42	Spicy Chicken Soup with Lemon Grass	57	25	17	0	1.5 VLMt, 1 Veg
43	Kabocha Spinach Soup with Beef	41	39	21	0	2 Veg, 0.5 MMt
44	Tortilla Soup	17	60	23	0	1.5 Veg, 0.5 St, 0.5 Fat
45	Chayote and Watercress Soup	25	54	21	0	1.5 Veg, 0.5 Fat
46	Lentil Soup	33	54	11	2	1 VLMt, 1 St, 1 Veg
47	Canadian Bacon, Cauliflower, Cheddar Cheese Soup	27	46	27	0	2 Veg, 0.5 MMt
48	Corn and Wild Rice Soup with Smoked Sausage	18	57	16	9	3 Veg, 1 St, 0.5LMt
49	Apple and Canadian Bacon Spinach Salad	27	53	19	0	1 Veg, 0.5LMt, 0.5 Fr
50	Garbanzo Bean and Chicory Salad	22	64	15	0	1.5 Veg, 1.5 St, 0.5LMt
51	Walnut Cheese Dressing	28	31	41	0	0.5 Fat
52	Mesclun of Greens with Banana Poppyseed Margarita Dressing	15	75	10	0	1 St, 0.5 Veg
53	Banana Poppyseed Margarita Dressing	9	85	6	0	0.5 Other
54	Watercress, Fava Bean and Radicchio Salad	16	73	12	0	1.5 Veg, 1 St, 0.5 Fr

* For ease of use, the percent of Calories from protein, carbohydrate, fat, and alcohol were rounded to use no decimal point, therefore the sum of the percents may occasionally total 99% or 101%.

** For some recipes, diabetic exchange values per serving were adjusted to more closely represent the actual Calorie, carbohydrate, protein, and fat content than strictly food-based exchanges.

Diabetic Exchange Abbreviations: Fr=Fruit; LM=Low-fat Milk, SM=Skim Milk; St=Starch; VLMt=Very Lean Meat, LMt=Lean Meat, MMt=Medium-fat Meat, HMt=High-fat Meat; Veg=Vegetable; Other=Other Carbohydrates; Fat=Fat Group; Free=less than 5 grams carbohydrates and 20 Calories.

Page		Protein	Percent Calories* From Carbohydrate	Fat	Alcohol	Diabetic Exchanges**
55	**SIDE DISHES**					
56	Fried Rice	17	69	14	0	2 St, 1 Veg
57	Brown Rice Confetti	9	83	7	0	1.5 St, 1 Other
58	Risotto* with Shrimp and Radicchio	21	57	14	8	2 Veg, 1 St, 0.5 VLMt, 0.5 Fat
59	Spanish Rice	10	81	9	0	2 St, 1 Other
60	Wild Rice Medley	11	83	6	0	2 Veg, 1.5 St, 1.5 Fr
61	Couscous Molded in Manoa Lettuce	14	84	2	0	2 St, 2 Veg, 1 Other
62	Mushroom Quinoa	16	71	13	0	2 Veg, 1.5 St
63	Lyonnaise Potato	7	81	12	0	1 St, 1 Other
64	Hawaiian Sweet Potato Cakes	12	75	13	0	2 Veg, 1.5 St
65	Duchess Potato in Tomato Halves	13	82	5	0	1 Veg, 0.5 St
66	Baked Potato Cakes	7	77	16	0	2 St
67	Grilled Curry Polenta	7	75	17	0	2 St
68	Farfalle (Bow-Tie) Pasta with Confetti Vegetables	14	81	5	0	2.5 St, 2 Veg
69	Thai Rice Noodles	10	80	9	0	2.5 St, 1 Veg, 0.5 Other
70	Carrot-Zucchini-Squash Wrapped in Spinach	15	47	38	0	1.5 Veg, 0.5 Fat
71	Steamed Swiss Chard	33	40	27	0	1.5 Veg, 0.5 Fat
72	Baby Bok Choy Oriental	29	38	33	0	1 Veg, 0.5 Fat
73	Braised Celery with Roasted Corn and Peppers	18	56	17	9	1 Veg, 1 St, 0.5 Fat
74	Lettuce Baked with Creamy Cider	23	56	21	0	1 Veg, 0.5 St, 0.5 LM

* For ease of use, the percent of Calories from protein, carbohydrate, fat, and alcohol were rounded to use no decimal point, therefore the sum of the percents may occasionally total 99% or 101%.

** For some recipes, diabetic exchange values per serving were adjusted to more closely represent the actual Calorie, carbohydrate, protein, and fat content than strictly food-based exchanges.

Diabetic Exchange Abbreviations: Fr=Fruit; LM=Low-fat Milk, SM=Skim Milk; St=Starch; VLMt=Very Lean Meat, LMt=Lean Meat, MMt=Medium-fat Meat, HMt=High-fat Meat;

Page		Protein	Carbohydrate	Fat	Alcohol	Diabetic Exchanges**
			Percent Calories* From			
75	Roasted Kabocha Squash	10	67	22	0	1.5 Veg
76	Candied Butternut Squash Casserole	4	84	12	0	2 Fr, 2 Veg, 0.5 St
77	**SEAFOOD**					
78	Ahi Salad with Champagne Vinaigrette	41	38	15	6	3 VLMt, 1.5 Veg, 1 Other, 0.5 Fat
79	Champagne Herbal Vinaigrette	5	47	1	48	free
80	Curried Monchong in Rice Wrappers with Cucumber Tomato Relish	47	29	24	0	3.5 LMt, 2 Veg, 0.5 Fr, 0.5 Fat
81	Cucumber Tomato Relish	7	37	56	0	free
82	Opah with Orange Mustard Glaze	45	28	27	0	3 VLMt, 1 Veg, 0.5 Fr, 0.5 Fat
83	Opakapaka* Florentine	58	19	24	0	3 VLMt, 1 Veg, 0.5 SM, 0.5 Fat
84	Poached Uku with Papaya Relish	77	9	12	2	5 VLMt, 1 Veg
85	Papaya Relish	3	78	1	18	0.5 Fr
86	Poached Whole Onaga with Wine, Caper, and Tomato Sauce	59	15	9	16	4 VLMt, 1.5 Veg, 0.5 Fat
87	Grilled Ahi with Miso Glaze and Grilled Vegetables	61	21	11	7	5 VLMt, 2.5 Veg
88	Striped Sea Bass Steamed in Chinese Tradition	63	18	16	4	3 VLMt, 1.5 Veg, 0.5 Fat
89	Nairagi Baked with Ricotta Cheese and Apple Banana	47	20	27	6	4 VLMt, 0.5 Fr, 0.5 SM, 1.5 Fat
90	Caramelized Halibut with Honey Dijon Cucumber Yogurt	60	23	17	0	4.5 VLMt, 1.5 Veg, 0.5 SM, 0.5 Fat

* For ease of use, the percent of Calories from protein, carbohydrate, fat, and alcohol were rounded to use no decimal point, therefore the sum of the percents may occasionally total 99% or 101%.

** For some recipes, diabetic exchange values per serving were adjusted to more closely represent the actual Calorie, carbohydrate, protein, and fat content than strictly food-based exchanges.

Diabetic Exchange Abbreviations: Fr=Fruit; LM=Low-fat Milk; SM=Skim Milk; St=Starch; VLMt=Very Lean Meat, LMt=Lean Meat, MMt=Medium-fat Meat, HMt=High-fat Meat; Veg=Vegetable; Other=Other Carbohydrates; Fat=Fat Group; Free=less than 5 grams carbohydrates and 20 Calories.

| Page | | Percent Calories* From | | | | Diabetic Exchanges** |
		Protein	Carbohydrate	Fat	Alcohol	
91	Honey Dijon Cucumber Yogurt	28	67	5	0	0.5 Veg
92	Shutome Made Easy	31	54	15	0	3.5 LMt, 2 St, 1.5 Fr, 0.5 Veg, 1 Fat
93	Fresh Water Prawn and Seared Scallops with Star Fruit and Saffron Cream	67	14	13	6	6.5 VLMt, 1 Veg, 0.5 Fr, 0.5 Fat
94	Star Fruit and Saffron Cream	6	33	21	40	free
95	Squid Simmered in Asian-Mediterranean Flavors	32	44	8	16	2.5 LMt, 4 Veg, 1 Other
96	Shellfish Bourride*	37	27	7	30	6 VLMt, 4 Fat, 1 St, 1 Other, 1 Veg
97	Shellfish Stock	1	10	1	89	4 Fat, 0.5 Fr
98	Buckwheat Soba - Sea of Japan	19	78	2	1	3 Other, 2 St, 1 Veg, 1 VLMt
99	Stir-Fried Shrimp with Peking Sauce	62	21	17	0	3 VLMt, 1.5 Veg
100	Lobster with Wine and Saffron Sauce	60	17	16	7	5.5 VLMt, 0.75 Other
101	**POULTRY**					
102	Szechuan Chicken Skewers	72	17	11	0	5.5 VLMt, 0.5 Fr, 0.5 Veg
103	Ikaika's Chow Fun	24	67	9	0	2.5 Veg, 2 St, 1 VLMt
104	Chicken Caesar Salad	22	58	19	1	2 St, 1 Veg, 1 VLMt, 0.5 Fat
105	Sweet and Sour Chicken Stir-Fry	37	57	5	1	3 VLMt, 3 Veg, 2 Fr
106	Chicken Beggar's Pouch Over Taro with Pineapple, Papaya, Poha Relish	20	70	10	0	3 Fr, 2 VLMt, 1 St, 1 Veg
107	Pineapple, Papaya, Poha Relish	2	96	2	0	0.5 Fr
108	Mango-Sauced Chicken	62	28	11	0	3.5 VLMt, 1.5 Veg, 0.5 Fr

* For ease of use, the percent of Calories from protein, carbohydrate, fat, and alcohol were rounded to use no decimal point, therefore the sum of the percents may occasionally total 99% or 101%.

** For some recipes, diabetic exchange values per serving were adjusted to more closely represent the actual Calorie, carbohydrate, protein, and fat content than strictly food-based exchanges.

Diabetic Exchange Abbreviations: Fr=Fruit; LM=Low-fat Milk; SM=Skim Milk; St=Starch; VLMt=Very Lean Meat, LMt=Lean Meat, MMt=Medium-fat Meat, HMt=High-fat Meat;

Page		Protein	Carbohydrate	Fat	Alcohol	Diabetic Exchanges**
			Percent Calories* From			
109	Mango Vinaigrette	5	92	3	0	Free
110	Honey-Shoyu Chicken	62	21	10	7	4 VLMt, 0.5 Fr
111	Chicken Curry Three Mushrooms	52	36	11	0	3.5 VLMt, 1.5 Veg, 0.5 Fr, 0.5 SM
112	Chicken Papaya, Pumpkin and Summer Squash	41	52	7	0	3.5 Veg, 1 VLMt
113	Apple Cider Chicken and Golden Raisins	49	40	10	0	4.5 VLMt, 2 Fr
114	Chicken Stew and Dumplings	33	53	14	0	2 VLMt, 2 St, 1 Veg
115	Dumplings	16	69	15	0	1.5 St
116	Capistrano Breast of Chicken	40	38	17	5	4 VLMt, 3 Veg, 1 Fr, 1 Fat
117	Chicken Cannelloni	29	56	15	0	3 St, 2 VLMt, 2 Veg, 0.5 SM, 0.5 Fat
118	Turkey Hungarian Goulash with Seasoned Parsley Egg Noodles	34	57	10	0	2 VLMt, 2 St, 2 Veg, 1 SM
119	Seasoned Parsley Egg Noodles	14	75	10	0	2 St, 0.5 Other
120	Turkey Cutlet with Cranberry Relish	52	40	8	0	4 VLMt, 1.5 Fr
121	Cranberry Relish	2	97	1	0	0.75 Fr
122	Chicken Marsala	52	22	12	15	3.5 VLMt, 1 Veg, 1 Fat, 0.5 Fr
123	Turkey Lasagna	32	43	25	0	2 VLMt, 1.5 St, 1 Veg, 1 Fat
124	Vermicelli with Turkey, Basil, and Plum Tomato	32	60	5	3	3 Veg, 3 VLMt, 2.5 St
125	**PORK, VEAL, BEEF**					
126	Roast Pork Loin with Dried Fruit Stuffing	36	43	20	2	3 VLMt, 1 Fr, 1 Veg, 0.5 St, 0.5 Fat
127	Shiitake Sauce	10	68	2	20	1 Veg

* For ease of use, the percent of Calories from protein, carbohydrate, fat, and alcohol were rounded to use no decimal point, therefore the sum of the percents may occasionally total 99% or 101%.

** For some recipes, diabetic exchange values per serving were adjusted to more closely represent the actual Calorie, carbohydrate, protein, and fat content than strictly food-based exchanges.

Diabetic Exchange Abbreviations: Fr=Fruit; LM=Low-fat Milk, SM=Skim Milk; St=Starch; VLMt=Very Lean Meat, LMt=Lean Meat, MMt=Medium-fat Meat, HMt=High-fat Meat; Veg=Vegetable; Other=Other Carbohydrates; Fat=Fat Group; Free=less than 5 grams carbohydrates and 20 Calories.

Page		Protein	Percent Calories* From Carbohydrate	Fat	Alcohol	Diabetic Exchanges**
128	Maple Rum Pork Medallions	42	31	23	4	3 VLMt, 1 Fr, 1 Fat
129	Ground Pork and Eggplant-Hunan Style	19	50	25	6	1.5 Veg, 0.5 VLMt, 0.5 Fat, 0.5 Other
130	Yu-Shiang Pork	44	31	22	3	3 LMt, 3 Veg, 0.5 Fr
131	Veal Piccata	23	59	14	3	2.5 St, 2 VLMt, 0.5 Fat, 1 Other
132	Veal Roast with Pear-Pepper Relish	54	18	20	7	4.5 VLMt, 1 Veg, 1 Fat, 0.5 Fr
133	Pear-Pepper Relish	3	94	3	0	0.5 Fr
134	Veal Scaloppine with Marsala	44	21	20	14	2.5 VLMt, 2 Veg, 1 Fat
135	Hilo Beef Stew	45	41	14	0	2.5 VLMt, 2 Veg, 1 St, 0.5 Fat
136	Poha Berry Beef Kebabs	30	44	26	0	3 Veg, 2 MMt, 1 Fr
137	Ginger-Pepper Beef	30	37	26	7	2 LMt, 1 Veg, 1 Fr, 0.5 Fat
138	Thai Beef with Lemon Grass and Thai Basil	26	54	20	0	2.5 St, 2 VLMt, 2 Veg, 1 Fat
139	Beef Broccoli with Oyster Sauce	54	26	20	0	4 VLMt, 2 Veg, 0.5 St
140	Beef Tomato	39	30	30	0	2 Veg, 1.5 LMt
141	Stuffed Cabbage	21	53	26	0	2.5 Veg, 1 St, 1 Fr, 1 MMt, 1 Fat
142	Paniolo Beef Braised in Beer	35	48	13	4	3.5 VLMt, 5 Veg, 2 St, 1.5 Fat
143	**VEGETARIAN DISHES**					
144	Vegetable Envelopes with Sweet Sour Sauce	12	77	12	0	4 Fr, 3 St, 2 Veg, 1 MMt
145	Yaki Soba with 7 Vegetables	13	74	13	0	4 Veg, 2 St, 1 Fr, 0.5 Fat
146	Vegetarian Chow Mein	8	74	16	2	1.5 Veg, 1.5 Other, 1 St, 1 Fat
147	Choi Sum with Oyster Sauce	10	82	8	0	3 Veg, 2.5 Other, 1 St, 0.5 Fat

* For ease of use, the percent of Calories from protein, carbohydrate, fat, and alcohol were rounded to use no decimal point, therefore the sum of the percents may occasionally total 99% or 101%.

** For some recipes, diabetic exchange values per serving were adjusted to more closely represent the actual Calorie, carbohydrate, protein, and fat content than strictly food-based exchanges.

Diabetic Exchange Abbreviations: Fr=Fruit; LM=Low-fat Milk, SM=Skim Milk; St=Starch; VLMt=Very Lean Meat, LMt=Lean Meat, MMt=Medium-fat Meat, HMt=High-fat Meat;

		Percent Calories* From			
Page	Protein	Carbohydrate	Fat	Alcohol	Diabetic Exchanges**
148	Tofu and Eggplant with Yellow Bean Sauce	21	57	23	0	4 Veg, 2.5 St, 1.5 MMt
149	Basque Garbanzo Stew	16	67	17	0	3 Veg, 1.5 Fr, 1 St, 0.5 SM, 0.5HM
150	Mediterranean Lentil Entree Salad	25	59	15	0	3.5 St, 3 Veg, 1.5 VLMt, 0.5 LM
151	Couscous Marseilles with Spinach, Mushroom and Walnuts	14	70	16	0	3 Veg, 1.5 Fr, 1 St, 1 Fat
152	Diamond Head Ratatouille	12	46	17	25	3 Veg, 1.5 Other, 1.5 Fat, 1 St
153	Soft Polenta	9	78	13	0	1.75 St
154	Eastern Indian Saffron Rice	12	78	10	0	3.5 St, 1 Fr, 1 Veg
155	Black-Eye Pea Calcutta	22	65	9	4	2 St, 1.5 Veg, 1 VLMt, 0.5 Fr
156	Eggplant Tamarind	9	75	16	0	2 St, 1.5 Other, 1.5 Veg, 0.5 Fat
157	Okra and Carrot Curry	12	74	14	0	3 Veg, 2 Fr, 0.5 Fat
158	Spicy Chili James Brian	24	68	7	0	2.5 Veg, 1.5 St, 0.5 VLMt
159	Stuffed Chayote with Mushroom and Tomato	15	67	19	0	2.5 Veg, 2 St, 0.5 Fat
160	Spaghetti Squash Ticker Tape Parade	12	76	12	0	3 Veg, 0.5 Fr
161	**DESSERTS**					
162	Chocolate-Macadamia Nut Biscotti	9	70	21	0	1 St, 0.5 Fr, 0.5 Fat
163	Lemon Bars	9	79	11	0	1.5 Fr, 1 St
164	Chocolate Zucchini Brownie with Triple Berry Sauce	8	88	4	0	2 Fr, 1 St, 1 Veg
165	Apricot Almond Taro Cakes	9	74	17	0	1 St, 1 Fr, 0.5 Fat

* For ease of use, the percent of Calories from protein, carbohydrate, fat, and alcohol were rounded to use no decimal point, therefore the sum of the percents may occasionally total 99% or 101%.

** For some recipes, diabetic exchange values per serving were adjusted to more closely represent the actual Calorie, carbohydrate, protein, and fat content than strictly food-based exchanges.

Diabetic Exchange Abbreviations: Fr=Fruit; LM=Low-fat Milk; SM=Skim Milk; St=Starch; VLMt=Very Lean Meat, LMt=Lean Meat, MMt=Medium-fat Meat, HMt=High-fat Meat; Veg=Vegetable; Other=Other Carbohydrates; Fat=Fat Group; Free=less than 5 grams carbohydrates and 20 Calories.

Percent Calories* From

Page		Protein	Carbohydrate	Fat	Alcohol	Diabetic Exchanges**
166	Orange Ice Grand Marnier	4	83	9	5	2 Fr
167	Nectarine and Wine Sherbet	8	84	2	6	2 Fr, 0.5 VLMt
168	Blushing Pears with Raspberry Sorbet	2	86	2	10	5.5 Fr, 0.5 Fat
169	Lychee Ginger Sorbet*	2	96	2	0	2 Fr
170	Warm Chocolate Pudding Parfait	17	73	10	0	1.5 Fr, 1 SM
171	Pistachio Rice Pudding with Rose Water	14	78	8	0	2 Fr, 1 St, 1 SM
172	Bread Pudding with Mandarin Orange Sauce	14	82	4	0	1.5 Fr, 1.5 St, 0.5 SM
173	Mandarin Orange Sauce	14	84	2	0	0.33 Fr
174	Peach and Apple Crisp á la Mode	8	88	4	0	2.25 Fr, 0.5 St, 0.5 SM
175	Breadfruit (Ulu) á la Mode	6	92	2	0	2.25 Fr, 0.5 SM
176	Apple Strudel	5	82	13	0	1.5 Fr, 0.5 St, 0.5 SM
177	Mango, Cranberry, Apple and Cherry Cobbler	5	92	4	0	3 Fr, 1 St
178	Watermelon Chiffon 4th of July	14	66	21	0	1.5 Fr, 0.5 VLMt
179	Baked Apples with Mincemeat en Phyllo	4	84	13	0	2 Fr, 0.5 St, 0.5 SM
180	Pumpkin-Pineapple Upside Down Cake	5	84	7	4	2.5 Fr, 1 St, 1 Veg, 0.5 Fat
181	Chocolate Strawberry Torte	7	85	8	0	2.5 Fr, 2.5 St
182	Chocolate Amaretto Souffle Torte w/ Raspberries	11	79	8	2	2 Fr, 1 St, 0.5 VLMt
183	Lilikoi Mousse	15	81	4	0	3 Fr, 1.5 VLMt
184	Baked Alaska with Triple Berry Sauce	12	82	6	0	2 Fr, 2 St, 0.5 SM

* For ease of use, the percent of Calories from protein, carbohydrate, fat, and alcohol were rounded to use no decimal point, therefore the sum of the percents may occasionally total 99% or 101%.

** For some recipes, diabetic exchange values per serving were adjusted to more closely represent the actual Calorie, carbohydrate, protein, and fat content than strictly food-based exchanges.

Diabetic Exchange Abbreviations: Fr=Fruit; LM=Low-fat Milk; SM=Skim Milk; St=Starch; VLMt=Very Lean Meat, LMt=Lean Meat, MMt=Medium-fat Meat, HMt=High-fat Meat; Veg=Vegetable; Other=Other Carbohydrates; Fat=Fat Group; Free=less than 5 grams carbohydrates and 20 Calories.

Percent Calories* From

Page		Protein	Carbohydrate	Fat	Alcohol	Diabetic Exchanges**
185	**BASIC RECIPES**					
186	Vegetable Stock	0	0	100	0	Free
187	Chicken Stock	47	0	53	0	Free
188	Fish Stock	3	4	1	93	2 Fat
189	Brown Rice	9	84	7	0	2.25 St
190	Jasmine Rice	8	91	1	0	3 St
191	Sweet and Sour Sauce	2	98	1	0	0.75 Fr
192	Marinara Sauce I	13	67	20	0	2 Veg
193	Marinara Sauce II	12	69	19	0	1.5 Veg
194	Roasted Garlic Paste	14	71	2	13	1.5 Veg
195	Pickled Ginger (Garni Shoga)	2	95	2	0	1 Veg
196	Chili Pepper Water	0	0	0	0	Free
197	Pastry Cream	22	77	2	0	0.25 Fr, 0.25 SM
198	Triple Berry Sauce	2	96	2	0	0.5 Fr

* For ease of use, the percent of Calories from protein, carbohydrate, fat, and alcohol were rounded to use no decimal point, therefore the sum of the percents may occasionally total 99% or 101%.

** For some recipes, diabetic exchange values per serving were adjusted to more closely represent the actual Calorie, carbohydrate, protein, and fat content than strictly food-based exchanges.

Diabetic Exchange Abbreviations: Fr=Fruit; LM=Low-fat Milk; SM=Skim Milk; St=Starch; VLMt=Very Lean Meat, LMt=Lean Meat, MMt=Medium-fat Meat, HMt=High-fat Meat; Veg=Vegetable; Other=Other Carbohydrates; Fat=Fat Group; Free=less than 5 grams carbohydrates and 20 Calories.

About the Authors

EXECUTIVE CHEF PATRICIA L. SALVADOR, CCC began her culinary career over 25 years ago at the Sky Chef and Naniloa Surf in Hilo, Hawai'i. She has held notable positions including Sous Chef at the Sheraton Princess Kaiulani, Executive Chef for Outrigger Prince Kuhio Hotel, and Personal Executive Chef for Doris Duke. She is co-owner of Fish & Poi Chefs. Chef Patricia Salvador was president and 1989 Chef of the Year for the American Culinary Federation - Honolulu Chapter. She holds numerous culinary awards, plaques, accommodations, and achievements, including Grand Prize for Hawai'i's Health & Fitness Expo '96 Competition.

EXECUTIVE CHEF AL SALVADOR, JR. began his cooking career in the U.S. Marines over 40 years ago. He has worked as Executive Chef at Ruths Chris, Parker Ranch Broiler, Kahana Keys on Maui, and restaurants in San Francisco East Bay Area. He is co-owner of Fish & Poi Chefs and is personal chef for a local celebrity. Al Salvador was vice-president of the American Culinary Federation - Honolulu Chapter and Chef of the Year for the American Culinary Federation - East Bay San Francisco, Kona-Kohala, Maui, and Honolulu Chapters. He holds numerous culinary awards, plaques, accommodations, and achievements, including 1976 Gold Medal Winner - Culinary Olympics, Frankfurt, Germany.

Their culinary expertise and 20 years of interest in eating more healthful has resulted in these wonderful recipes.

DR. JOANNIE DOBBS graduated in dietetics from Michigan State University and holds a Ph.D. in nutrition from the University of California at Davis. She is a Certified Nutrition Specialist (C.N.S.) who has worked in food and nutrition for more than 25 years. As sole proprietor of Exploring New Concepts, Joannie is a consultant to restaurant chefs and food companies, and does nutrient analysis for various publications. She is co-author of the recent cookbook, *Bone Appetit*, developed for the Hawai'i Osteoporosis Foundation and co-writes the column "Health Options" for the *Honolulu Star Bulletin* newspaper. Joannie is also a member of the American Culinary Federation-Honolulu Chapter.